Treasure Island

Bryony Lavery's plays include *Her Aching Heart* (Pink Paper Play of the Year 1992) and *A Wedding Story* (2000). Her play *Frozen*, commissioned by Birmingham Repertory Theatre, won the TMA Best Play Award, the Eileen Anderson Central Television Award, and was then produced on Broadway where it was nominated for four Tony awards. She also wrote *Last Easter*, produced in The Door, and created adaptations of *Uncle Vanya* and *A Christmas Carol* as an associate artist for The REP. *Stockholm*, with Frantic Assembly, won the Wolff-Whiting award for Best Play of 2008. Recent work includes *Beautiful Burnout* for the National Theatre of Scotland and Frantic Assembly, which received a Fringe First at Edinburgh; *The Believers* with Frantic Assembly at the Theatre Royal Plymouth and the Tricycle; *Kursk* with Sound and Fury at the Young Vic and Sydney Opera House; *Cesario* for the National Theatre; *Thursday* at the Adelaide Festival; *Queen Coal* at the Studio, Sheffield; and an adaptation of *Tales of the City/More Tales of the City* by Armistead Maupin for BBC Radio 4. Forthcoming work includes stage adaptations of *101 Dalmatians* for Chichester Festival Theatre; *Brideshead Revisited* for York Theatre Royal; and *Picnic at Hanging Rock* for ETT/Brink. Bryony Lavery is an honorary Doctor of Arts at De Montfort University and a Fellow of the Royal Society of Literature.

from Faber by the same author

BRYONY LAVERY PLAYS ONE
(*A Wedding Story, Frozen, Illyria, More Light*)

MORE LIGHT
SMOKE
LAST EASTER
BEAUTIFUL BURNOUT
BELIEVERS

Treasure Island

a play by
BRYONY LAVERY

adapted from the novel by
ROBERT LOUIS STEVENSON

FABER & FABER

First published in 2014
by Faber and Faber Limited
74–77 Great Russell Street
London WC1B 3DA

Typeset by Country Setting, Kingsdown, Kent CT14 8ES
Printed and bound in the UK by CPI Group (UK) Ltd, Croydon CR0 4YY

A CIP record for this book is available from the British Library

ISBN 978-0-571-32436-1

2 4 6 8 10 9 7 5 3 1

Treasure Island in this adaptation was first performed
on the Olivier stage of the National Theatre, London, on
3 December 2104, with the following cast:

Jim Hawkins Patsy Ferran
Grandma Gillian Hanna
Bill Bones Aidan Kelly
Dr Livesey Helena Lymbery
Squire Trelawney / Voice of Parrot Nick Fletcher
Mrs Crossley Alexandra Maher
Red Ruth Heather Dutton
Job Anderson Raj Bajaj
Silent Sue Lena Kaur
Black Dog Daniel Coonan
Blind Pew David Sterne
Captain Smollett Paul Dodds
Long John Silver Arthur Darvill
Lucky Micky Jonathan Livingstone
Joan the Goat Clare-Louise Cordwell
Israel Hands Angela de Castro
Dick the Dandy David Langham
Killigrew the Kind Alastair Parker
George Badger Oliver Birch
Grey Tim Samuels
Ben Gunn Joshua James
Shanty Singer Roger Wilson
Parrot Ben Thompson

Director Polly Findlay
Designer Lizzie Clachan

Lighting Designer Bruno Poet
Music Dan Jones and John Tams
Sound Designer Dan Jones
Fight Director Bret Yount
Movement Jack Murphy
Illusionist Chris Fisher
Music Supervisor Matthew Scott
Music Director Theo Jamieson
Comedy Consultant Clive Mendus
Creative Associate Carolina Valdes
Company Voice Work Jeannette Nelson
    and Daniele Lydon
Staff Director Sam Caird

Characters

ADMIRAL BENBOW INN

Jim Hawkins
a teenage girl dressed like a boy

Grandma Hawkins
a landlady who cannot spell

Doctor Livesey
a doctor and magistrate

Squire Trelawney
a squire with a big mouth

Mrs Crossley
drinker and churchgoer

Red Ruth
future crew member

Job Anderson
future crew member

Lucky Micky
future crew member

Silent Sue
future crew member

Jem
replacement Jim

Shanty Man
a singer and musician

VISITORS

Bill Bones
haunted villain

Black Dog
eight-fingered villain

Blind Pew
blind villain

CREW OF THE HISPANIOLA

Captain Smollett
captain

Long John Silver
one-legged cook, charmer and villain

Joan the Goat
headbutter

Israel Hands
clumsy Brazilian

Dick the Dandy
pirate voguist

Killigrew the Kind
gentle killer

George Badger
malcontent

Grey
a grey, forgettable character

Captain Flint
a parrot

ISLAND INHABITANTS

Ben Gunn
marooned cabin boy

TREASURE ISLAND

For Polly Findlay
*princess of plotting and all the pirate crews
of her wonderfully creative workshops*

'No man is an island, entire of itself;
every man is a piece of the Continent,
a part of the main.'

John Donne

TREASURE

noun 1 wealth stored or accumulated, esp. in the form of precious metals, gold and silver coins

noun 2 a store of anything valuable

noun 3 anything valued and presented as precious

verb to hold or keep as precious

The odd line lengths
weird   spacing
and plethora of exclamation marks
and question marks in the text
are the author's attempt to convey
the frenetic nature of these characters
in their situation!!!

In the text / indicates one character
talking over another

Act One

ONE
AN INN

Song: 'Bright Morning Star'.
Black Cove, south-west England.
Above us, all the stars of the northern hemisphere in
the incredible darkness of eighteenth-century England . . .
Under the sky . . .
On the world's edge . . .
Jim Hawkins Junior . . .
A teenage girl in boy's attire . . .

Jim
Bright morning star a-rising
Bright morning star a-rising
Bright morning star a-rising
Day is a-breaking in my soul

Men   various
Have chosen *me* to tell *you*
From *beginning* to *end*
Keeping nothing back but its *bearings*
All the particulars about Treasure Island . . .

(*Crows and rooks caw . . .*)

The bitter spiteful winter both my parents died –

(*A spectacularly old lady, Grandma, enters . . . pats*
Jim on the head or something fond . . .)

Before I could read this bright page above us
My old Grandma and I –

Grandma
Not so much of the 'old'!

Jim
    – ran the Admiral Benbow Inn
    Above Black Cove

    (*A fire blazes into being . . .*)

Grandma (*crossing with loaded tray*)
    Head-In-Dreams!!!
    W-E-R-K!
    Work!!!!

    (*Grandma, crossing on another innkeeping chore,
    reveals, thrillingly . . .* THE ADMIRAL BENBOW INN *. . .
    a perilously precarious place of drink, hideable nooks
    and hard drinking . . .*)

Jim
    However Grandma spelled it!!!!
    I *hated* W-E-R-K

    (*And Jim multitasks as . . .
        Old, overused things break for her as . . .*)

    On the very *coldest* of days
    With no *food* in my belly

Grandma
    Or in *mine*

Jim
    The *First* arrived
    And the *terrible* dreams began.

TWO
THE FIRST

*Arriving from a far distant perspective with a large sea
chest . . . Bill Bones . . .*

Bones (*to the awful choir in his head*)
    Don't sing!

(But the terrible singing continues . . .)

Don't sing in my head!!!

(Sees Jim.)

This is a pleasant-sittyated grog shop.
And a handy cove.
Much company, mate?

Jim
Precious little.

Bones
What's your name, swab?

Jim
Jim Hawkins, Sir.

Bones
Be you boy or be you girl?

Jim
That be *my* business.

Bones
Then this be *my* business
This is the berth for me.
Get my sea chest and stow it *safe*.

(Although a spectacularly old woman, Grandma lifts the heavy huge sea chest with ease . . .)

Grandma
Paying Guest!!!
Thank you, Heavens!!!

Bones
I'm Billy Bones
I'm a plain man
Rum, bacon and eggs is what I want

(He spies . . .)

And that head up there to watch the road *thiswards*
And ships arriving *thatwards* . . .

(*Grandma stows the chest high in the inn . . .*)

Jim

Yes, Mr Bones

Bones

Yes, *Captain*

Jim

Yes, Captain

Bones

That

(*He throws down three or four gold pieces . . .*)

For my vittals and grog, Jim Hawkins.

(*Grandma dives for the money . . .*)

Grandma

And food for *us*, Jim!

(*Bones seizes Jim in a painful grip . . .*)

Bones

Tell me, if ye dare, when I've worked through
Keep a weather eye open
always
for a seafaring man
with *one leg*
and let *nothing at all* near that chest!

(*He looks out to sea, along the road, everywhere . . .*)

Grog!

Jim

Yes, Captain!
He stays
He drinks

In all weather foul or fair
From dawn's earliest light
Through all the long hard day
To darkest night
We watch the road
Like hawks   like *eagles* . . .
The sea
for a one-legged man
so long so hard so   *afeared*
I begin to see this one-legged ghoul in my dreams!

Grandma
Head-in-Clouds!

(*Ordinary customers have appeared suddenly in the inn.*)

Paying Customers!!!

Squire
Claret, Jim Hawkins.

Red Ruth
Bread, Jim Hawkins!
My stomach thinks my throat's been cut!!!

Mrs Crossley
I'll take a tiny Glass of / 'Ladies' Delight'

Doctor
Ginever! Large One!
I've delivered *five* babies today /
Three surviving!

Job Anderson
Lemonade!

Several
Lemonade???

Job Anderson
My Old Lady said   after last Saturday's shenanigans –

(*General mutter signifying 'Yes, we remember Saturday's shenanigans'.*)

'Drink one more drop of your damn *downfall*, Job Anderson,
I'll *kill* ye!!'

(*General mutter signifying 'We know His Old Lady always keeps her word'.*)

Grandma
Anything for *you*, Lucky Micky?

Lucky Micky
Cider!
Whole Pint!
(*Holding up a coin.*) Just found this –

Job Anderson
Whole groat!

Lucky Micky
– in a cowpat!!!

(*Wipes it on his sleeve , holds it out . . .*)

Job Anderson
Lucky *again*, Lucky Micky!!!

Lucky Micky
Luckiest Man in All Black Cove!
And whatever Silent Sue wants!

(*Silent Sue tries to order . . .*)

Grandma
What will it be, Silent Sue?

(*Silent Sue mimes and gesticulates . . .*)

Ginever?
Porter?
Cider?

(Specific mime to Red Ruth which means . . .)

Red Ruth
Silent Sue says she'll have *a Ladies' Delight,*
Mrs Hawkins!

Bones
Grog!

(All heads look to him.
All look back to their drinks and heads down!
Grandma and Jim work and serve customers as . . .)

Jim
He stays
He Drinks *mightily*   and
Watches *always*   for this one-legged seafaring man
Who now *lives* in my nightmares!
I think how he might have lost his leg!!!!
I think if his leg is separated from his body . . .
Where lies that leg??????
Or was he always a monstrous kind of creature who
   never had but one leg
And that
In the middle of his body!

(As she works . . .
Some nightmarish appearances of one-leggedness . . .)

Grandma
JIM!
Folks is thirsty!
T-H-U-R-S-T-Y!
Large Brandy, Doctor Livesey . . .?
It's medicinal . . .

Doctor
It's not, Mrs Hawkins
But *yes.*

Jim

See him
Bounce and pursue me over hedge and ditch!

Grandma

Brandy, *BrainGone*!

Bones

Sing me to distraction, would ye?
I'll sing *ye* to distraction!
These *landlubbers* will drown your voices!!!
Sing!
'Fifteen men on the dead men's chest
Yo ho ho and a bottle of rum . . .'

Damn you all, *Sing or I'll cut ye!*

All (*sing, bullied*)

'Drink and the devil had done for the rest –
Yo ho ho and a bottle of rum'

(*Until Squire slaps a fist on the table.*)

Squire

Stop that *infernal* racket!
I cannot hear myself *drink*!

(*Bones slaps his hand on his table.*)

Bones

Sing!

Squire

Silence!

Bones

Sing!

Squire

Silence!!!!

(*Some competitive fist-thumping until Bones rises and
crosses to stand over the Squire . . .*
   Between them, with jug, Jim . . .)

Jim (*whispers*)
Squire Trelawney was Black Cove's *second* most
frightening fellow

Bones
I've lived my life among the wickedest men that God
ever allowed on the sea . . .
Do not cross me!

Squire
Were you addressing me, Sir?

Bones
I *was* addressing you, Sir!

Squire
One word, Sir
If you keep on drinking rum,
The world will soon be quit of a very dirty rascal

(*Bones draws a huge knife.*
Puts it to Squire's throat . . .)

Bones
Sing!!!

Squire (*singing, a bit quavery*)
'Fifteen men on a dead / man's chest . . .'

(*Others join in.*)

'Yo ho ho and a bottle of rum'

(*With an even bigger fist pound, Doctor erupts . . .*)

Doctor
Silence!!!
I cannot hear myself drink!!!
Cease this '*yo- ho-hoing*' INSTANTER!!

Jim (*whispering*)
The Doctor was Black Cove's *first* most frightening
fellow

Doctor
If you do not put away that knife *this instant*
I *promise*
You shall *hang* at the next assizes!

(*Battle of looks.*)

Hang, Sir!
By your astoundingly filthy *neck*, Sir!
Until your face turns *blue*
Until your tongue *swells* and *blackens*.
Knife!!!

(*Bones, cowed, puts away his knife.*)

I will have an eye upon you day and night.
Pour.

(*Jim pours.*
  Squire back, almost valiant, with . . .)

Squire
I'm Squire Trelawney
I'm the damn *magistrate* here!
If I catch a breath a *breath* of complaint against you
I'll have you hunted down
And strung as high as the stars in the night sky!

(*Squire and Doctor drain their drinks, exit.*
  Bones slaps his head . . .)

Bones (*quieter*)
Still the terrible singing!!!
More Grog!!!!

(*He slaps down his tankard.*
  It, being old, breaks . . .)

Jim

Bill Bones bid fare to ruin us
Staying week after week
Driving away our few customers
The money all exhausted . . .

Grandma

He's supposed to be a '*Paying*' Guest!

Jim

He's getting *Free* dinners

Grandma

And Us *No* dinner!!!

Jim

Let's *demand* our rightful money. Grandma!!!

Grandma

Good Sir, the matterofthepaymentoftheroomthebacon /
theeggsthe grog . . .

Bones

My chewing tobacco, / Jim!

(*She fetches it as . . .*)

Grandma

Whichstatesinbigclearwritingtheoutstanding / owed . . .

Bones

My snuff, girl.

(*Jim fetches it . . .*)

Grandma

Sir . . . This girl and me's had nor supper nor breakfast!
N-O-R-T *nought!*
SeeSirifyoudon'tpayus*fairwe* don't eat and then we
goes all weak and cannot carry your *grog* / to you!!!

Bones

More grog!

Grandma

This girl's fetching and carrying for you for *free*.

(*Moving tableau of . . .*)

In the shoes she's had from her –

Both

– poor dead father!

Jim

All this unpaid for, *hurry* Captain!

Bones

Who will hurry *here?*
The one-legged one????
Cutlass!!!

(*Jim fetches cutlass.*
Bones brandishes it dangerously . . .
Jim and Grandma duck.)

What will he have in his hand????

(*Duck again . . .*)

A *Dagger?*

The *Black Spot??????*

(*Somewhere, lurking, a one-legged man . . .*)

The clever varmint knows *stars*!
His infernal brain will navigate him *thiswards*
I must not sleep!

(*He watches thiswards and thatwards . . .*
But sees not the one-legged nightmare . . .
As Grandma sweeps up some dismembered legs . . .)

FOUR
THE SECOND ARRIVES

Jim

He *sleeps* not
He *pays* not

Grandma

So *We* Eat not!

Jim

Then
Like dirt gathering in a corner . . .
The *second* arrives.

(*Black Dog, pale, tallowy, appears in the gloom.*)

Two legs but
I feel my heart grow *chill* . . .

Black Dog

I'll take a rum
Lad
Lass?

(*He beckons with his left hand . . . on which two fingers are missing . . .*)

Jim

He was wanting two fingers on his left hand!

Black Dog

Come here whatever you be.
Come very nearer here.

Jim

But two legs so . . . she nears him . . .

Black Dog

Where's the favoured drinking berth of my mate Bill?

Jim

This is the Captain's favoured spot, Sir

Black Dog
The 'Captain' is it? La di da!
Cut on one cheek?

(*Jim nods.*)

Mighty pleasant way with him *particular in drink*?

(*Jim nods.*)

Here?

Jim
Upstairs, Sir

Black Dog
Upstairs is it?

(*Bones descends stairs as . . .*)

You and me'll just go into the *shadows*

(*Lifts Jim by collar so feet barely skim the floor . . .*)

And we'll give Bill a little surprise

(*Draws his cutlass . . .*)

Bless 'is dark traitoring heart

(*Bones arrives, Black Dog reveals . . .*)

Ah-ha *Bones*!

Bones
Ah-ha *villain*!!

(*Like dogs on point . . .*)

Black Dog
Come, Bill, you know an old shipmate surely

Bones
Black Dog

Black Dog
As ever was
You took some running to earth, old shipmate

Bones

Here I am, *shipmate*

Black Dog

Mate no longer
Since *I* lost these two talons!
I'll have a glass of rum from this dear child here
As I've took such a liking to
And we'll sit down and talk square.
None of your *keyholes*, Girl!!!
Now Bill . . .

Bones

Now, Black Dog . . .

(*Two shipmates sit to conduct a quick and combative
whispered conversation . . .*
    Grandma and Jim eavesdrop . . .)

Black Dog

You *knows* what I wants, Bill!

Bones

I knows *exactly* what you wants, Black Dog!
What's *my* share

Black Dog

What's *my* share too!
Where's *Flint's Fist, Billy?*

Bones

Safely hid from *you,* Black Dog.

Black Dog

Be warned, Bones . . .
I got most of *our old Walrus crew*
lying off Black Cove in a tidy lugger
grievous disappointed you *still* think it's *your* share
when you just thieved it and ran!

Jim

What is *this* about?

Grandma

Not *bill settling*!

(*Whispering becomes more heated and audible . . .*)

Black Dog

I *advise* you for your *health* . . . don't keep us / swabs
waiting, Billy Bones . . .

Bones

And I advise *you*, Black Dog . . . Flint's Fist is *mine*

Black Dog

Is *ours*!

Bones

Not so!

Black Dog

Yes So!

Jim

Flint's Fist, what's that????

Black Dog

We're *done* asking *nicely*
Hand over *Flint's Fist . . . fingers and thumb*
Or . . . it's the Black Spot for you!

Bones

Or the Red Blood for you!

(*Both up and standing nose to nose . . .*
  Horrible dirty fight . . .
  In which Black Dog gets Bones against a pillar . . .)

Black Dog

Flint's Fist . . . where????

(*They fight up the stairs.*
  Black Dog has Bones pinned to the bed . . .)

Tell, or ye die *unpeaceful* in bed *instanter*!!!

(*Bones escapes, runs downstairs, where Black Dog gets him on a table.*)

Cough, villain!

(*Bones throws him off with . . .*)

Bones
Bleed, villain!!!

(*Black Dog in full flight, blood streaming . . .*)

Black Dog
This for all Betrayers!!!

(*Exits . . . A last blow from him splits an inn upright in two pieces . . .*
    The world starts to list . . .)

Bones
I am discovered!
Get my sea chest!
I must get away from here . . .

(*But his body betrays him . . . He crashes to the floor.*)

Grandma
Get Doctor Livesey!

Jim
The Doctor was, fortuitously, just then arriving.

Doctor (*checks Bones' unconscious pile of flesh*)
Raise his foul freeloading head!

(*They do.*)

Grandma
Doctor!
Some *black art* has struck him down!

Doctor
Some *Black Art*???

Peasant Nonsense!
Scoundrel's had *a stroke.*
We must do our best to save this fellow's very
    worthless life
Jim! Holding receptacle!

(*Jim finds something not quite appropriate to hold.*)

Afraid of blood?

Jim
No Sir.

Doctor
Then, hold the receptacle *firm.*
Mrs Hawkins, open the rogue's shirt . . .

(*A bag full of terrible early medical appliances
    Doctor selects the most gruesome and opens a vein.
    Red blood spouts and gushes . . . Bones comes to . . .
Bones in full fight mode . . .*)

Bones
Where's Black Dog?????

Doctor
There is no *black dog* here
You have had a stroke
And *I* have just
dragged you headforemost out of the grave

Bones
Get me a grog / girl . . .

Doctor
No More Grog!
Jim, keep this *utter fool* from the poison which will
    snuff him
Out like the brief candle all men really are!

(*Exits with bag.
    Jim and Grandma prop up Bones . . .*)

Jim

My nightmares now were all of *Flint's Fist*!
What was it?
It's terrifying!!!!
Was it . . . a *severed hand* with *no arm attached!*

(*A hand on her shoulder from behind.*)

Aaagh!

(*It proves to be the hand and arm of Bill Bones . . .
with the horrors, impossible to control . . . clamped
horribly on to Jim . . .*)

Bones

Grog!!!!

FIVE
A TERRIBLE ISLAND IN THE BRAIN

Jim

No grog!!!!

(*Bones hurls Jim about like a sock puppet . . .*)

No!!!

(*Bones bursts into tears . . .
    An impressive display of acute suffering . . .*)

Bones

Look how my fingers *fidgets*!
If I don't have grog
The *horrors* will recommence their *singing* . . .
Sleep has left me, Jim!
Living men will pursue you
But *Ghost* men are the ones who *catch* you!
If I close my eyes
I am *bobbing* off that *terrible* island

Jim

Island?

Bones

With Flint *Flint!* upon it . . . *singing*
I am *cold* inside to think of Flint *singing*
Grogin hereGirl!!!

(*Holds out his goblet.*)

Jim

I'll get you grog on *one* condition . . .

Bones

Name it!

Jim

You answer my *questions*!
Stop my nightmare imaginings

Bones

Done!

(*Jim fetches bottle, but keeps it, despite all Bones'
valiant and ingenious attempts to get it out of his
grasp . . .*)

Grog!

(*Jim pours a very small tot
Bones drains it off.*)

Grog!

Jim

Question!!!
What is Flint's Fist?

Bones

I cannot tell ye that!
Grog

Jim

No

(*And she successfully keeps the bottle from Bones.*)

Bones
Jim!
Please!
My *whole body* fidgets . . .

(*Until . . .*)

Flint's Fist . . . unlocks *a secret* . . . shhhh!
The island will hear me . . .
More I cannot say!

(*Reaches for bottle but Jim holds it away . . .*)

Jim
Then Who was Flint who was *Flint*?

Bones
The ghost who sings *always* in my head!
The dead captain of a terrible ship!
Grog!!!

(*Jim pours a tot. Bones drinks . . . holds out his goblet for more.*)

Jim
What ship? What ship????

Bones
The bloodsoaked *Walrus* of course!
Ten there was left on board
Six there was, went with Flint upon that island

(*Bones whimpers, Jim advances the bottle a bit . . .*)

Jim
What Island . . .???

Bones
Never speak out loud of *The Island!!!*
It *Listens Always!!!*

(*Some island sounds . . .*)

Six set out all-a-singing . . .
(*Sings.*) 'Fifteen men on a dead man's chest . . .'
Aaaahhhh!

(*Bones clutches his head.*)

But only *Flint* came back!

Jim
What *happened* to the six?????

Bones
Yes, Jim . . . *what* happened to the six . . . ?

(*Counts off on his fingers . . .*)

McGraw . . .
Allardyce . . .
O'Doherty
Thimble the Sail Mender?
. . . that scrawny *cabin boy*?
Grimes the Giant . . . Grimes *the Giant*???? . . .
All vanished!!!!!

Jim
Did *Flint* butcher *all six* . . . ?

Bones
Or was it something
(*Whispered.*) on that terrible island?????
Grog, Jim

Jim
Question!
Who is the one-legged man you watch for?

Bones
He is the very *devil* himself!
Watches and listens me all quiet like the island itself!!!
Grog!

Jim

Question!
What is the Black Spot?

Bones

It is the thing that will enter my head and heart and
take me through the doors of hell!

(*And he forces Jim's hand to pour . . .*)

Stop singing in my head!!!!

Jim

And he watches thiswards and thatwards
And   I do too

(*And they watch, terrified . . .*)

SIX
THE THIRD ARRIVES

Jim

Until
A bitter foggy frosty afternoon
A *terrible* sound . . .

Grandma

Oh H-E-L,   what *now*?????

Jim

The *Third*!!!!!

(*A weird terrifying approaching tapping . . .*
    Blind Pew . . . blind, tapping before him with a
stick . . .
    Immensely tall, immensely terrifying and with no
eyes . . .)

Pew

Will any kind friend inform a poor blind man

Who has lost the precious sight / of his eyes
In the gracious defence of his native country England
And God bless King George . . .

Jim

A *dreadful* figure . . .
But *two* legs, so . . .

(*She nears him.*)

Pew

Where or in what part of this country he be?????

Jim

You have Black Hill Cove at your back
The Admiral Benbow Inn before you

Pew

I hear a *young* voice
Will you give me your hand and lead me in?

(*Jim holds out his hand.
    Blind Pew grips it like a vice and pulls him close.*)

Now . . . *boy?*

Blind Pew fumbles at her . . .

Jim

Girl! Stop!

Pew

Take me to the captain

Jim

I dare not

Pew

Take me in straight
Or I'll break your arm

(*An awful wrench.*)

Jim

Aaargh!
Sir
The captain sits with *a drawn cutlass*

Pew

Come now, *march.*
Lead me to him.
When I'm in view
Cry out
'Here's a friend for you, Bill'
If you don't . . .

(*Even more awful wrench.*)

Jim

Aaargh!

(*In to Bones, terrible acting . . .*)

'Here's a friend for you, Bill.'

Bones

Blind Pew!!!!

(*Bones tries and fails to rise . . .*)

Pew

Now Bill
If I can't *see* you, I can hear *a finger stirring*
Hold out your left hand.
Boy or Girl, take his left hand by the wrist and bring
    it near my right

(*They both obey him.*)

You came not of your own account to *us*
We come to *you* . . .
Your last chance to serve us fair, Bill Bones

Bones

Be damned to all of you!!!

Pew

Then here you are.

(*He passes something to Bones' hand.*)

I will return
With your old shipmates from the *Walrus*
By   ten o'clock
Discover whether there be any sailor's honour left
    in you . . .

(*He closes Bones' hand round . . .*)

And now that's done

(*He exits, tapping . . .*
    Jim watches Bones, who opens his hand, sees what's there.
    Bones feels something snap in his brain.)

Bones

Get my . . .

(*He feels something stop in his chest.*)

Oh Jim . . .

(*Then, with a peculiar sound*
    Crumples horribly to the floor . . .)

Jim Grandma!!!!!
Wake him *up*!

Grandma (*she can't*)
He's dead!!!
D-E-D.

Jim

I do not *at all* like people *dying*!

(*She opens out Bones' hand . . .*
    Goes quite still.)

The *Black Spot*
It has taken him through the doors of . . .
Oh, *Grandma* . . .
Blind Pew said they return *at ten o'clock.*

(*Inn clock strikes . . . six beats . . .*)

Some *terrible* villains want *something*

Grandma / Jim
Which will be in his sea chest!

Grandma
We have four hours!

Jim
We should just *R-U-N*, Grandma!

Grandma
N-E-V-A!
Our *neighbours* will help us against these varmints . . .

(*But the inn is deserted except for Mrs Crossley,
finishing her Ladies' Delight . . .*)

That pile of evil bones owes us, Jim!!!
I will *not* lose money that belongs to my poor hungry
    fatherless motherless shoeless girl!

Jim (*goes and finds a very rusty pistol*)
Mother's pistol!

(*Tries it. It falls into three pieces . . .
    They put it back together again as . . .*)

(*Not bravely.*) Here we will stay!
And . . . small thanks to all *chicken-hearted drinkers*!

Grandma
We'll have that *chest* open
I'll thank you for that bag, Mrs Crossley
To put our lawful money in!

Mrs Crossley

    I have *a chicken* in this bag, Mrs Hawkins.

Jim (*points mother's pistol*)

    We'll thank you for that bag, Mrs Crossley

    (*And cocks it . . .*

        Mrs Crossley hands over the bag . . .

        Jim opens it . . . A live hen clucks out, which Jim
    hands to Mrs Crossley . . .)

    You get your church bag *back*, Mrs Crossley

    If you bring back here *anyone*

    Who will save an honest landlady / and her
       granddaughter!

Grandma

    Try the Doctor . . . try Squire Trelawney / A*nybody.*

Mrs Crossley

    Don't get it over all *bloody* when they *kill* you!

    It's my *church* bag!!!

    (*Exit Mrs Crossley, bladdered, with hen . . .*

        Dark is falling . . .

        Owls hoot

        Grandma lights a candle . . .

        To the chest . . .)

Grandma

    Locked!

Jim

    String round his neck!

    Key!

Grandma

    Unlock! *Unlock!*

    (*Jim unlocks chest then . . .*)

Jim

    You open the *chest*, Grandma . . .

(*Grandma opens the chest very, very carefully . . .*
A terrible smell of putrefaction.
A weirdly coloured cloud of steaming noxious air
rises menacingly . . .)

Grandma
Jim *you* . . .

Jim
Grandma . . . *your turn*!

(*Together, they look in the chest . . .*)

Old account book . . . all stained
Papers . . . / various . . .

Grandma
What?
Any / thing?

Jim
Old bills . . .
(*Reads one paper.*) 'McGraw's drinks total owed'.
(*Shows to Grandma.*) It's a huge amount!
(*Reads another.*) 'The Collected Love Ballads of Donal
    O'Doherty' . . .
Lock of yellow hair . . . These are his fellow crew on
    the *Walrus*.

Grandma
Nothing to pay his damn bill?

Jim
No

Grandma
Put them with the kindling
At very least Bill Bones will light our fire and *warm* us.

(*And Jim places the papers ready to blaze as . . .*
Grandma finds a huge glove, puts it on.)

Giant Glove!!! Pointing Upwards!

Jim

Giant *Grimes*!

Grandma

Something in it!!!

Jim

Flint's Fist . . .????

(*Grandma finds most frighteningly . . .*)

A finger!!!
Flint's finger?????

Grandma

That won't buy us bread!

Jim

The finger was arranged pointing upwards . . . to
the . . .

(*Jim examines the lid.*)

Grandma . . .
I think this . . .
may be a *false* lid!!!

(*She rips it . . . coins cascade down . . .*)

Grandma

Here's *Coin*!
Flint's Fist is but a Big Glove pointing to a Big Hand
of coin!!!
We could be rich on this, Jim!!!

(*They are both tempted . . .*)

We could buy a little cottage, *big* cottage, hens . . .
Sit down forever . . .

Jim

I could see Grandma was sore tempted . . .
But . . .

Grandma
   I'll show these rogues I'm an honest woman
   His outstanding bill
   Not a *farthing* more!
   These coins are of all countries but *England* . . .
   Hold out Mrs Crossley's church bag, Jim

   (*Tap tapping . . .*
      They freeze with terror.)

SEVEN
THE NEXT HORRORS ARRIVE

Jim
   Blind Pew.

   (*Tapping draws nearer, strikes sharp on the inn door.*)

   (*Whispers.*) It's not *ten* yet!

Grandma (*whispers*)
   Cheating Lying Scum!

   (*Handle turned.*
      Bolt rattled furiously.
      Utter silence.
      Tapping recommences . . . drawing away.
      A whistle code from every direction . . .)

   Take the money and run
   I am very S-K-A-R-D . . .

   (*She faints dead away . . .*)

Jim (*whispering*)
   Grandma . . .
   Grandma!!!! . . .
   Oh no no no no no no no . . .

   (*Jim hides her . . . folds her up . . . somewhere
   impossible . . .*)

35

Yes yes yes yes yes . . .

(*Realises she too needs to hide.*)

Oh no no no no nono . . .

(*Hides herself somewhere equally impossible . . .*)

Yesyesyesyesyes!!!

Pew (*from outside*)
Down with the door

Door shattered . . .
Framed . . . completely unrecognisable . . .
Black Dog, Joan the Goat, Dick Dandy, Killigrew the
Kind, Badger, Israel Hands . . . all faces covered with black
masks and with terrible weaponry and sea lanterns . . .
They are faceless, spooky and utterly terrifying!

Pew In in in!!!!

Black Dog
Bill's *dead* the very *disappearing devil*!

(*Joan the Goat's favoured weapon and search tool is*
the headbutt . . .)

Joan
Dush dush *dush!*
Dammeblasttarnationzounds swamp-it!
Old Bill Bones is now just *bones*!

Pew
Search around him
Rest of you scatter about and find his *chest.*

(*Israel Hands falls over something . . .*)

Hands
Ai! Ai! Desculpa aí! Merda! [Whoops! Damme!!!]

(*Dick and Killigrew scatter. Empty chest . . .*)

Pew Is it there?

Dick
The shining money's there!!!

Pew
Curse the *money*!!!!
I mean *Flint's Fist*!

Killigrew
We don't see it.

(*And, with his huge hands, crumbles something to sawdust . . .*
Israel Hands falls over something . . .)

Hands
Desculpa ait Merda! [Whoops! Sorry!]

Badger
A-hiding our rightful share!
That's Typical o' Bill Bones!

Joan
VillainSwineSwabsRoguessBlaggardingDamnation!!!!

(*And she headbutts Grandma's chair to matchsticks in exasperation . . .*)

Dick
Is it *on* Bones?

(*A horrid group pick-up and shaking of Bones' dead body . . . Badger has a handy cosh . . .*)

Badger
Nutthin!!!

Pew
Some swab's *took* it for his own!

Killigrew
We met no swabs leaving here . . .

(*All go still.*)

Badger
  Regard!!!!!

  (*They all regard . . . a lit candle . . .*)

  They left their *glim* here and . . . !

Black Dog (*touches it*)
  Villain!!! . . . Still hot!

Pew (*whispers*)
  Here *still* then!!!
  Take the hovel apart!
  Anyone you find . . . bring *herewards*!

  (*A scary search through the inn . . .*
      Cutlasses thrust into door panels . . . narrowly
  missing Jim and Grandma . . .
      Jim resourceful, villains murderous . . .
      A far-off whistle sounds once.
      All freeze.
      More whistles . . .)

Dick
  Lugger sounding the alarm . . . Pew –

Pew
  Search *faster*!!!

  (*And a speed-up of cutlass thrusting, inn-destroying*
  search and heroine/Grandma danger as . . .)

Hands
  Desculpa ait Merda! [Ouch! Sorry! Fell!]

Joan
  Listen!
  Blaggarding BloodyDamnationableHorses!

Black Dog
  Galloping *lugger*wards!!!

Killigrew

We'll have to *budge,* mates
His Majesty's Navy is closing in!!!

Pew

Oh shiver my soul
If I had eyes!
We'll be rich as *kings* if you find it!

Black Dog

There's doubloons here!

Pew

Doubloons is *nothing* to *Flint's Fist*!!!
Search faster!

(*More acceleration . . .*
Sound of approaching horse hooves . . .)

Badger

Horses!

Black Dog

Nearing thiswards!!

Dick

His Majesty's *Army* now!!!
Time to board ship!

(*And they depart . . . mostly over and through Pew.*
Pew strikes about with his stick . . .)

Pew

Lead me out, lead me out!
Shipmates! Friends! . . . you won't leave old Pew,
    mates, not old Pew.

(*But they leave, in which somehow –*
Blind Pew is impaled on his own stick and moves
no more.
The inn is much less of an inn . . .)

THE CAVALRY (SORT OF) ARRIVES

Jim unpacks Grandma from her hiding place . . .

Grandma
My *chair*!
Pigs!
P-I-G-Z!!!!

(*Doctor with Mrs Crossley . . . with hen, burst in tooled up . . .*)

Doctor
All here sound and hearty???

Jim
All well but the Captain . . . and . . . *him* . . .

(*Squire bursts in, even more tooled up . . .*)

Squire
Lugger's gone!
Skedaddled!
Damn and Blast!!!
What did they take?

Jim
Nothing!
They just *left* the coins!!!
Pew said 'Doubloons is *nothing* to Flint's fist' . . .

Grandma
The night is cold through all these *holes* . . .
I'll start the fire . . .
Perhaps a brandy . . .

(*Common folk follow Grandma for drink as . . .*)

Mrs Crossley
I'll thank you for my church bag, Mrs Hawkins . . .

Grandma
Mrs Crossley . . .

Mrs Crossley
I won't be staying, Mrs Hawkins.
You've rather upset my *laying* hen.

(*Bag returned, Mrs Crossley takes it, stows upset
laying hen. Both exit with dignity . . .*)

Doctor
They left *the coins*.
All this murderous pursuit
And they left *the coins*.

Squire
Odd.

Doctor
Most odd.
Not after *small* reward.
Not after *money*.
Well then
What in *fortune* were they after?

Jim
Look!

(*Written on the chest . . .*)

'Edward Flint his chest.
Of all chests most beautiful most secret and most best.'

Doctor
Terrible poetry!
Who in all *damnation* is Edward Flint????

Squire
Flint????
Doctor, do you never read a *newspaper???*
Captain Flint was

The *bloodthirstiest* buccaneer that ever sailed!
Butchered his enemies like they were *pork chops*!
His ship the *Walrus* was the Worst Nightmare of
The Seven Seas!!!
His *crew* on the Walrus a pack of *wolves* not *men*! . . .
Blackbeard was a *child* to Flint!
He was *the Devil in Human Flesh*
That's who *Flint* was!

Jim
Bones was no captain he was a common *thief*
This is not his chest at all!
Flint's *Chest* and 'Flint's *fist*'

Doctor
What in *heaven* is Flint's *Fist?*

Jim
Sirs . . . 'secretest' . . . Flint's *chest* has *hidden bits* . . .

Doctor
Then let us examine the chest carefully . . .

(*Squire uncarefully upends the chest.*)

Squire!!!

Grandma
There's the brandy . . .

(*Puts it down . . . proceeds towards . . .*)

Now . . . a nice warm fire . . .

Squire
Nothing of *worth*!
Damme!

(*Grandma stacks kindling . . .*)

Doctor
This chest contained *absolutely nothing more* . . .????

(*Grandma pokes old papers into the kindling . . .*)

Jim
Nothing, Sir . . .
But what you see before you . . .

(*Grandma strikes a good flame on her tinderbox . . .*)

And . . .
The old bills and such which Grandma put to light
the fire . . .

(*A pause . . .*
Then . . . as one . . .)

All
Grandma!!! / Mrs Hawkins!!! / The papers! The papers!
Don't use it *to light the fire!!!!!!*

(*Jim rescues the papers from the flames in the absolute*
nick of time . . .)

Jim
I believe, Squire . . .
The thing I have here must be *Flint's Fist* . . .

Squire
I'll take it

Doctor
I'll take it!

(*Doctor picks up the papers, turns them over . . .*
All but Jim put on their spectacles . . .)

This is the blackhearted hound's *account book* . . .
'Flint – Captain . . . Bill Bones – First Mate!'
The names of ships *scuttled* . . .

Squire (*snatches it, reads*)
'*Silver Swan* – Off Palm Key he got itt'
'The *Unicorn* – Offe Caracas he gott it'

'The *Golden Deer* – right in Havana port he got itt!'
Blaggardly Bloodletting Pirates!!!

(*Jim examines the chest as . . .*)

Doctor
Then . . .
a list of sums . . .
Then . . . 'rightful shares'.
Flint . . . Bones . . .
Pew . . . Black Dog . . . . . . descending amounts then –

(*Jim taps walls and then base of chest.*)

Squire
'Rest of crew . . . equal parts the rest'

Jim
Sirs . . .
If the coin was in a false *lid* . . .
Perhaps the chest contains also
A false *bottom* . . .?

Doctor
Care / ful . . .

Squire
Yes!

(*He uncarefully rips the secret bottom open . . .*)

What's *this* . . .?

Doctor
Some sort of oiled skin . . .
Small   folded many times . . .

(*They open it out . . .*)

Squire
It's a drawing of something . . .

(*They examine it . . .
  Turn it . . .*)

Doctor
Of . . . *an island* . . .?

Jim
. . . The island that *listens*!!!

(*This is scary . . .*)

Bones speaks . . . (*Points to Bones' body.*) spoke of this
island before the Black Spot killed him.

(*They dial to a whisper . . .*)

Squire
Something written on the back!!!!

Doctor
It's a *ditty* or something . . .
(*Reads.*) 'So I may always find my pile.
Lat E 62 17 20 Long NE 19 3 40 will find the isle . . .'
Shocking scansion . . .

Squire
Coordinates *coordinates*.

Jim
Isle! It *is* an island!

Doctor (*reads on*)
'The heart protected by the ribs
Who knows this will get his dibs
Upon it
If unfair of face
It's simple
Escalate the biggest pimple . . .'
This line should hold *eleven syllables* . . .
'Upon that spot I suggest you linger
Until you see a pointing finger . . .'

Squire
It's a clue it's a clue . . .

Doctor (*reads on*)
  'Stand thereupon
  Chose moon or sun
  The cove as knows to turn his face
  Has wit and luck to find the place.'

Squire
  Oh my Heavens, it's . . .

Doctor
  'By my hand. Edward Flint.'

Squire
  . . . It's a treasure map
  By Heavens . . .
  It's a treasure map!!!!!
  A treasure / map!!!!! It's a treasure map!!!!

Doctor
  Squire!!!!
  Stop *dancing*!
  Shhhhhhhhh!!!!!

  (*Back to whispering . . .*)

  There are *common* men and women *drinking!*
  You are so confoundedly hotheaded and
    exclamatory!!!
  Treasure . . . *yes*
  But . . .
  Will *any* treasure amount to more than *home* / and
    happiness . . .

Jim
  Yes!

Squire
  Amount, Doctor Stay-at-home????????
  It will *amount* to this
  Fit out a ship

I'll take you and clever-at-solving-problems! –
   Hawkins here along

Jim
   Yes!

Squire
   And Red Ruth and Silent Sue and Job Anderson and
   Lucky Micky particularly *Lucky* Micky and I'll *have*
      that treasure !!!!
   We'll *all* have that treasure!!!

Jim
   Yes, we'll *all* have that treasure!!!!
   Buy cottages! And hens! And *shoes*!

Squire
   I'll get me servants to packmysummerlinenmybrandy
      tobacco!!!

Doctor
   But . . .

Squire
   Livesey
   You will give up this wretched practice *at once.*

Doctor
   Well, that's all / very . . .

Squire
   I start for *Bristol NOW!!!*
   In three weeks – *two* weeks – *ten* days
   We'll have the best ship –

Doctor
   Yes but . . .

Squire
   The *choicest* crew
   You *ship's doctor*
   I   *admiral!!!*

Doctor
You'll follow with Jim here
She's not afraid of blood! blaggards! fire!

Jim
Anything!

Squire
She'll be cabin boy/girl/either/*both*!

Jim
We'll have favourable winds, a quick passage!

Squire
Not the *least* difficulty in finding the spot because

Jim / Squire We have a treasure map!!!

(*They pretend to dig, pick-axe . . .*)

Jim
Then
Money to *eat*

Squire
To *roll* in!!!

Jim
To *wear!!!*

Doctor
Trelawney
I'll go with you

Jim
I'll go with you!

Grandma
You *won't*!

Jim
I *will*!

Doctor
Girls need adventures too, / Mrs Hawkins.

Grandma
Nice quiet *safe* ones here *at home!*

Doctor
There's only *one* man I'm afraid of

Squire
Name the dog

Doctor
You
Squire!
You *cannot* hold your tongue!
Blurdiblurdiblur the livelong day!!!!
We are not the only ones who know this

Jim
No

Doctor
The less than *human Walrus* crew who attacked this
    inn just now

(*She medically checks Blind Pew's lifeless body . . .*)

Those left *alive*
Are one and all
Panting and slavering after the treasure

(*Snatches the map.*)

I will keep this map not *you!*
Not *one* of us must breathe a word of what we've
    found

Squire
Doctor
You are *always* in the right of it.
I'll be silent as the grave!

NINE
JOURNEY TO BRISTOL

Song: 'Blood Red Roses' (violin, Shanty Man and company.)

Me boots and clothes they're all in pawn
   Go-down!
You blood red roses
   Go-down!
And it's mighty draughty round Cape Horn
   Go-down!
You blood red roses
   Go-down!
Oh! You pinks and posies
   Go-down!
You blood red roses
   Go-down!
I thought I heard the old man say
Just one more pull and then belay

TEN
CREW-HIRING

The inn disappears . . .
   Seagulls shriek and scream as . . .
   On the edge of the world's sea . . .
   Sitting, nearby, a gentle harmless man in a long coat, glasses on, apparently two-legged, reading a newspaper: Long John Silver . . . but we don't know this yet . . .
   Doctor and Jim arrive, with apple barrel.

Jim
I was soon in *BRISTOL!!!!!!*

(*Showing off her new Adventure Outfit.*)

In Father's Breeches! Mother's *Sunday* Chemise!
Doctor's second-best shoes!!!!

Doctor

We must load this apple barrel!
I have an unproven notion that *apples* eaten daily
    hold preventative properties . . .

(*Squire arrives with landlubbers from togging-up
shopping trip . . .*)

Squire

You have arrived!!!
Stand here ready, men!
Dear friends,
The ship is bought and fitted.
You never imagined a sweeter schooner
A child might sail her!
Two hundred tons
Her name
Hispaniola
She lies two miles out there at anchor
Ready for sea

(*Captain enters . . .*)

I have appointed a Captain named . . .

Captain

Smollett. Captain *Smollett*!!!
What is going on here, Sir?

Squire

I have been hiring crew for our ship like a true Ruler
    of the Waves!!!

Captain

You've been *hiring crew* for *my ship* . . . ?

Squire

My ship, Captain . . .
I have already with me Job Anderson, Red Ruth,
Silent Sue and Lucky Micky . . .

(*Red Ruth, Job Anderson, Silent Sue, Lucky Micky in a tight clump . . . with exciting new kit! . . . and varying degrees of anticipation . . .*)

Red Ruth
Well *this* ain't Home, Squire!
This ain't *ploughing!!!!*

Lucky Micky
Seagull just shat on my head!
That's *lucky*!!!

Job Anderson
What do you think of all this then, Silent Sue?

Red Ruth (*translating Silent Sue*)
Big Water! New Jersey! Socks!!!
Smashing!!!!

Captain
These (*bad*) peasants   and (*worse*) women are my
   crew, Sir?

Squire
Are *my* crew, Sir.
All from my own estate
All *utterly* reliable and . . .

Captain
Can they actually *sail* a ship, Sir?

Squire
Well, you're a captain, *you* can *instruct* them how
   to sail a ship, Sir!
Follow the captain, fellows!
Captain Smollett will soon have you shipshape!!!

Captain
I'm *the captain* of the ship, Sir.
I appoint the crew.

Squire
I'm *paying* for the ship, Sir.

I appoint them.
Crew So Far . . . Follow the captain!

(*Captain walks, incandescent and purple with rage, up the gangway to his ship, followed by variously eager novices.*)

Jim! Doctor, follow My Crew!
I must continue my Sailor-Hiring.
Recruiting anyone else is proving devilish slow . . .

(*Jim and Doctor board as . . .*)

Jim
Ship!!!
Schooner!!!!
A child might sail her!!!!

Doctor (*sees sea for first time*)
Oh Lord, all this sea!!!! (*Not a fan of.*)

(*Jim and Doctor's departure has revealed Grey.*)

Squire
Ah!
Experienced sailor at last!
Name?

Grey
Grey, Sir.

Squire
Grey
Hired
Stand ready.

(*Grey stands. Squire paces . . . No one arrives . . .*)

Sailors?
Able Seamen?
Damme, where *is* everybody????

(*He sits down next to Long John Silver . . .*)

Silver
Beautiful ship out there, Sir.

Squire
The *sweetest* schooner, Sir.
Sailor, Sir?

Silver
Was, Sir
But . . .
Injured in my country's service
I have no pension

Squire
The *abominable* age we live in!
In pain, Sir?

Silver
Only when I think about the lack of pension, Sir.

(*Both laugh.*)

Lovely day
Smell that salt, Sir . . .

(*Both take in the good sea air.*)

Both
Aaaah . . .

Silver
What are *you* doing here, Sir?

Squire
Hiring *a crew* . . .
And finding it devilish difficult, Sir . . .

Silver
Difficult Sir, why Sir?

Squire
It's as if all seafaring men hereabouts are *scared*
of something, Sir . . .

Silver

I'd *heard* that, Sir
For I know *all* seafaring men in Bristol . . .

Squire

I wish you knew of any *willing* seafaring men in
Bristol, Sir

Silver

Not if you're a-taking men into mortal danger, Sir . . .

Squire

I'm taking them after *treasure,* Sir!

Silver

Quiet, Sir!
The world *crawls* with large-eared villains!
And . . .
Treasure has a way of getting *smaller* the more it
is exposed to the air . . . Hold your secrets *close* . . .

Squire

This is good counsel, Sir
I will not tell *a soul*!

Silver

Keep your treasure's bearings to *yourself.*

Squire

Keep the island's bearings to *myself.* Good!

Silver

And . . . Take provisions *aplenty* . . . I've heard that
Treasure is devilish hard to *find* once you are in its
vicinity

Squire (*very quietly*)

Not if you have a map, Sir

Silver

Sir, tell *no one* you have a map!
Treasure makes even Englishmen *mad*, Sir . . .

Squire

More good counsel!

Thank you, Sir, but I'm *apparently* too big *a blabbermouth*
  to keep the map!

The map is with *my soon-arriving friends*!!!

Silver

Very wise, Sir.

We *open-hearted* gentlemen are just too –

Both

Open!

(*Some open, gentlemanly laughter.*)

Squire

Well, Sir, I'd better be about my business . . .

A crew won't assemble itself

Silver

If only I could help, Sir . . .

But . . . It's been a long time since I was in a seafaring
  way . . .

Let's think . . .

(*He whistles to help himself think . . .*
    The tune is 'Fifteen men on a dead man's chest . . .'
    Suddenly seafaring types start to arrive out of the
  shadows as . . .)

Well, where has *these lot* come from?????

Squire

What a most remarkable stroke of fortune!!!!

I know not *how* you conjured them up . . . but

Look   such an assortment of . . .

Suddenly

Between us

We got together a crew

Of the toughest old salts imaginable . . .

Silver
Killigrew

Killigrew
The *Kind,* Sir . . .

Silver
Effective in the getting of *fresh* meat while at sea, Sir.

Killigrew
Mackerel, sprats, seagulls, rats
Just the *once* an Albatross

Silver
Soft but *strong* hands . . .

Killigrew
Meat always acquired in the *kindest* possible manner . . .

Squire
Love Fresh Meat!
Hired!

Dick
Dick
. . . The Dandy

(*Dick reties his bandanna artfully . . .*)

You may be *at sea*
You may be *in salt*
But seafaring's no excuse for *sloppy.*
This (*trimming*) is Bristol Bombazine!
This (*outfit*) is Newport Nankeen!
That's the *without*
As for the *within*

(*Opens coat, reveals a splendid and various collection of sharp knives.*)

Observe how I got my daggers *disported . . .*

(*Order . . .*)

Slicer gutters thrusters *short* finisher *long-distance*
  finishers
That's in The Frenchie Style!!!
Look and Lacrimate!

Silver

Tidiness . . . Important in a good crew, Sir . . .

Squire

You're right, Sir.
Hired!

Silver

Joan the Goat.

Squire Joan the . . .?

Joan

Broke my head in two pieces on the hard deck in a sea
  fight, Sir
A *very good friend took* his favourite stewpot lid his
  favourite stewpot lid!!! . . .
Heated it redhot on his stovetop
Welded it round Fashioned it
Nailed it to my skull for a brand new cast-iron
  foreheadbrandnewcastironforehead . . .
See? You can knock on it if ye like it won't ever
  break everdushdushdush!
Bar occasional *crippling* headaches . . .
I'm right as rain . . .
Right as *rain*

Silver

The Poor Woman's brain needs some good sea air, Sir.

Squire

Simple Human Kindness!
Hired!

Joan
Dush!

Hands (*in Portuguese*)
Sou Israel Hands! [I am Israel Hands.]

Silver
Here's Israel Hands . . .
For First Mate, Sir

Squire
A *foreigner*???

Silver
But *honest.*

(*Hands puts out his hand to shake, drops his bag . . .*)

Hands
Sou um pouco desajeitado! [I'm a bit clumsy.]

Silver
He's a *bit* clumsy.

Hands
Nasci embaixo de uma estrela desajeitada.

Silver
Born under a far-off clumsy star, Sir.

(*Hands picks up his bag but drops it on Squire's feet.*)

Hands
Foram me dadas essas maõs desajeitadas –

Silver
He was given these clumsy hands –

(*Hands' feet slip accidentally . . .*)

Hands
E tambem estes pés desajeitados!

Silver
Also two clumsy feet.

Squire
A clumsy sailor . . . I'm not sure . . .

Hands
*Mas eu sou um bom navegador e minha mãe
bençoada me deu esta medalha sagrada então nem
a minha falta de jeito e nem nenhum mortal pode
me matar.*

Silver
But he is a fine navigator and his blessed mother has
given him a sacred medal so neither his clumsiness nor
any mortal man can kill him.

Squire (*moved*)
I had a mother too . . .

Silver
Lash him to the wheel
He's golden

Hands
Ouro puro!

Squire
Hired.

Silver
Black / Dog –

Black Dog (*disguised . . . in gloves*)
Black *Cat*, Sir.

Silver
My mistake . . . Black *Cat*, Squire . . .

Black Dog
Come very nearer here, Sir.
Black *Dogs* in general mean that death is very near.
Black *Cats* on the *other* hand means good fortune
    is very nearer . . .

(*Two butter-wouldn't-melt smiles . . .*)

Squire
Hired!
Next!

Silver
George Badger

Badger
Considered last as usual!
It's not fair

Squire
It's not.

Badger
I don't like this captain . . .

Squire
Nor *me,* Sir.
Hired!

(*Badger moves to reveal Grey . . .
And then there's . . .*)

Oh!
And . . . ?

Grey
Grey, Sir.
You already hired me, Sir.

Squire
Grey!

Silver
Never seen *this one* before!!!

Grey
Nobody ever remembers / me . . .
Grey by name, Grey by nature . . .

Squire

Blackguards *everyone*
None of 'em pretty to look at . . .
But men and women by their faces
Of the most *indomitable* spirit.
Get on board, rest of crew!

(*Rest of crew board and disappear . . .*)

I declare we can fight *a frigate*

Silver

Then it's back to my landbound job a-cooking the
best stew in Bristol . . .

Squire

I have not hired a cook!
Good friend . . .
How can I persuade you to come along on our
adventure . . . ?

Silver

I care not for money I care not for gold . . .
But . . .

(*It is a terrible, quite long internal struggle . . .*)

I do *love* a ship beneath my feet
The wind at my back
And the *stars*   a-twinkle-and-a-telling above me!
Perhaps . . . an easy job in the galley . . .

(*More internal struggle.*)

I'll come cook for you, Sir!

Squire

Then, let's *shipwards*
I feel like the First Sea Lord!!!
I have found a *crew*
A *cook*
And a *new friend*!

(Squire follows. Half way along the gangway he turns.)

Tell me . . . stout friend . . .
What should I call you?

Silver
When I'm a-*cooking* . . . they call me
Barbecue

Squire
Barbecue!

(And on to the ship . . .)

Silver
And
When I was up on deck . . .
With the stars above me . . .
They called me *Long John Silver.*

(He stands, comes forward . . .
  He has only one leg.)

Captain Flint!

(His parrot, a dark strange bird, magically there . . .)

Flint
Pieces of eight!
Pieces of eight!
Pieces of eight!

(. . . attaches itself to Silver.)

Silver
Couldn't have said it better meself, Bird!

(Together parrot and pirate board the ship.)

Song: Making Leave

Our ship went a-sailing out over the bar
  Way down Rio!

We pointed her head to the old Southern Star
And we're bound for the Rio Grande!
   Haul! on the bowlin'
So early in the mornin'
   Haul! on the bowlin'
The bowlin'
   Haul! on the bowlin'
Before the day is dawnin'
   Haul! on the bowlin'
The bowlin'
   Haul!
Little Sally Racket
   Haul 'em away!
Pawned her father's jacket
   Haul 'em away!
Then she went and lost the ticket
   Haul 'em away
To me ho-de-hido
   Haul 'em away!
Take her by the scruff now
   Haul 'em away!
Never treat her rough now
   Haul 'em away!
And that'll be enough now
   Haul 'em away!
To me ho-de-hido
(*Entire Crew.*) *Haul 'em away!*

ELEVEN
MY BEAUTIFUL SHIP!

A wonderful ship has assembled before our eyes . . .
Song: 'Blood Red Roses'. Then . . .

Captain
   Sail us out, Bosun.

Black Dog

Heave away capstan

(*Shanty Man leads 'Haul Away' / 'Little Sally Ratchet'*
work songs . . .)

Away headline
Away bowline
Up top ratlines!!!!
Anchor sighted and clea
Set mainsail
Set staysail
Set topsail!!!

(*And we are sailing!*)

Jim

Oh how I *love* my ship!!!!
My *Hispaniola*!
My ship!
I love you, ship!!!!

(*And runs to the captain's cabin as . . .*
   Cries of pelagic birds, storm petrels, guillemots,
skuas, terns . . .)

TWELVE
TWO CAPTAINS, ONE SHIP

Captain and Jim enter captain's cabin . . .
   Squire and Doctor have drink and food on the
Captain's chart table.

Captain

Clear this landlubbery picnic from my table, Sirs!!!
This is the *place* with the *chart upon it* from which
I am *navigating* this vessel, Sir!
I am of the mind to turn for home!

Squire

And *I* have a mind to lower a boat and let you go!

Doctor

Squire . . . can you / just . . .

Squire

What is turning you beetroot *this / time*, Captain?

Captain

Firstmost . . .
I should have had the chosing of my men!

Doctor (*to Captain*)

Yes, you should, Captain . . .
(*To Squire.*) *Squire LeapybeforeLooky!*

Squire

What is *wrong* with the crew I have chosen?

Captain

Secondmost, your landlubbers
know *not* how to be on a ship!

(*In the sleeping quarters, Job Anderson and Silent Sue.*)

Job Anderson

Look at this fancy sleeping beds, Silent Sue!

(*They get in one side, fall out the other of their very narrow bunks.*)

Squire

But they have been trained to hard toil by *me* and are quick to learn!

Captain

Thirdmost
We are living in confined spaces, *not fields*!!!

(*In the galley, Red Ruth turns round with a large side of beef, knocks down a lot of pans, turns the other way, knocks down Grey.*)

Red Ruth
This place ain't big enough to swing a cow!

Captain
Ships are dangerous places . . .
They need to know the danger spots . . .

(*Silent Sue stands in a circle of rope on deck . . .*
It tightens round her ankle . . .
Black Dog, on the other side of the deck from her,
hoists, she is suspended upside down, her mouth open
in a silent scream.)

Squire
They are most intelligent for unschooled men!!

(*A flying fish comes through a porthole . . .*
Lands right at Lucky Micky's feet.)

Lucky Micky
Flying fish!
Look at them colours!!!
I'm gonna nail that on my wall!!!

(*He does this . . . water spouts into his face.*)

I made a *face washer*!
Lucky Micky!

Captain
Fourthmost
I hear from your *bumpkins*, those who can *speak!!!*
we are going after *treasure.*
They *know* you have a map of an island.
I do not know *who* has this map.

Squire
Doctor Livesey / has it . . .

Doctor / Jim
Squire! Shhh!!!!

Captain

It must be kept from *everyone*.

Doctor

Captain, *I* will hide it somewhere *safe* . . .

Squire

Yes!

Treasure makes even English men and women *mad* . . .
They lose their reason, their loyalty, their *morals*

(*Squire hands Doctor the map . . . Doctor exits.*)

Captain

Fifthmost

All Crew and You Cease all this *treasure talk instanter!*

Squire

Sixthmost, I think the *worse* of you . . .

Captain

Seventhmost, I think the worse of you!
Ship's *boy*

Jim

Girl!

Captain

I'll have no favourites on my ship!
Galley!
Help The Cook!
Belay!

(*Jim exits cabin, descends to the galley . . .*)

Jim

I am *quite* of the Squire's thinking,
I hate the captain *deeply*!

THIRTEEN
COOKING

Jim, in galley, bangs pots and pans . . .

Jim

'Belay!'
Cooking!!!
I might as well be *at home!!!*

(Something or someone in the dark there . . .)

Cook?
Hello?
Cabin girl here!

(She sees in the galley . . . the dark, amazing Parrot.)

Hello! . . .
Who are *you . . .?*
What fine feathers!
May I touch them, handsome Sir?

(Parrot is beyond adorable and cute . . .)

You're the most beautiful bird I've ever seen!!!
Better than Mrs Crossley's hen!!!

Flint

Pieces of eight
Pieces of eight
Where's the pieces of eight?

Jim

Oh, you *talk!!!!*
Say something *more,* beautiful Sir . . .

(Silver is in the doorway . . .)

Silver

What more would you like him to say . . .?

(Jim turns . . .)

Jim

And there was *my nightmare*.
The one-legged man!

(*Jim seizes the first utensil she can find which is a fork.
Holds it out . . .*)

Silver

Going to *fight* me, are you?
Then   You're actually better with a *knife*
And . . . don't come at me *frontwards* . . .
Because . . . see . . . it's so easy to *disarm* you . . .

(*Disarms her. Hands her a knife instead.*)

Here, take it, then . . .
Wait till I'm turned, see . . .

(*He stands with his back to her.*)

Then you may sink your blade deep into my liver

(*Points . . .*)

Right *there* . . .

(*Starts chopping herbs as . . .*)

Go on. Send me to my seat in heaven . . . be nice not
to be hopping round no longer . . .

(*She stands with her knife. He's still got his back to her.*)

Did the *lonely* leg scare you?

Jim

Yes

Silver

Or . . . the one that's *not* there?

Jim

The ghost leg
Yes.

Silver

Ghosts *best* you where live men *can't*   but
You mustn't be frightened of one-legged men . . .
    not at sea . . .
Sailing's a *dangerous* game . . . . . . truly . . .
You'll find a one-legged man on near every ship that
    sails the sea.

Jim

Truly?

Silver

Cross my heart and hope to die.
You lose your leg, you pays doubloons and gets a
    better one!

(*Introduction of terrifically brilliant prosthetic leg . . .*)

And you go from deck to galley
From sailor to *cook* . . . *Girl.*
And a pretty one too, right Captain Flint?

Jim

Captain Flint was a *pirate* and a *scoundrel*

Silver

Was indeed.

(*He puts his chopped herbs into a pot . . .*)

This parrot's a pirate and a scoundrel too.
Pretty but always *pilfering*, aren't you, Bird?

Flint

Where's the pieces of eight?

Silver

And where's my *peanuts* as was on this table, pirate?

(*Parrot stares at him.*)

I'm Long John Silver
Cook

Jim
Jim Hawkins
Cabin girl

(*Silver brings a spoon and bowl of stew . . .*)

Silver
Do me a kindness. Try my stew.
It'll *warm* you

(*Jim tries it.
    It is truly delicious.*)

Aye . . .?

Jim (*as she eats*)
Aye!

Silver
First time away from home?

(*She nods, homesick.*)

First time at sea?

(*She nods, lonely.*)

First time not knowing where you are?

(*She nods, vulnerable.*)

And a strange *one*-legged man frightens the life out
of you!

(*She nods because he understands this.*)

Never mind . . . I hear you're after treasure

Jim
Who told you that?

Silver
My friend the Squire.
I *pray* that map he mentioned's safely stowed . . .?

Jim
Oh yes!

Silver
Where?

Jim
Somewhere secret!

Silver
And do you know the secret . . .?

(*Beat.*)

Jim
If I knew the secret, it wouldn't be secret, would it . . .?

Silver
You're young
But you're smart as paint
Help me with these vegetables, Cabin Girl . . .

(*And they both fall to stereo-maestro chopping as* . . .)

Jim
I began to see this one-legged man Silver
was a fine judge of character!
He understood, better than Grandma even,
my need for continuous large amounts of food . . .
His galley as we worked –

Silver
Pass me that pig sausage, Jim . . .

Jim
– was warmer, cosier than My Inn . . .

Silver
Stand by the oven, Girl . . .
this north-easterly's finding its way through all the ship
today!

Jim

He knew everything about my ship . . .

Silver

If a ship is like the horse of the sea
the captain's cabin is the very brains of it . . .

(Cut to map room.
 Israel Hands, bringing an appropriate armful of
maps to the Captain, drops them . . .)

Jim

He was the easiest of masters . . .

(Silver feeds Parrot, then Jim, a piece of apple . . .
unlike the Captain.
 Cut to beetroot Captain . . .)

Captain

Maps on the Map Table you Brazilian Butterfingers!!
Not on The Infernal Floor!
A Captain navigates from Maps on the *navigating*
 table not Maps on the Floor you Striped Idiot!!!

Hands

Abierda, Mi Capitano! Furioso!!

Silver

and that sea horse is always walking trotting a-canter
gallop across the sea towards its destination . . .

(Cut to Doctor, a bit bilious. in medical area, with
Joan the Goat on table, Lucky Micky, Dick the Dandy
assisting . . .)

Doctor

Oh . . . this terrible motion . . .
when does it ever get *still????*
bleeuerrr . . .

Silver

best place for the ride on your sea horse is abaft the
mast . . .

(*Cut to Squire's cabin.*
Squire ordering, Badger assisting.)

Squire

Look here . . .
My dressing gown is damp.   Damp Damme!

Badger

That's ships for you . . .

Squire

And look here!
My French Brandy Keg is tilting!
French Brandy needs to lie still!

Badger

That's sea for you

Silver

Even on ship the world's an unequal place . . .
you and me Jim . . . bottom of the pile . . .
with the worst of billets!

Jim

Squire shouldn't complain!

Silver

but he's Squire Squealer . . .

Squire (*squealing*)

Its not good enough!

Badger

Not fair not fair at all

Squire

Not good enough by a long chalk!!!

(Silver oinks and squeals in Squire register . . .
Jim likes this . . . joins in.)

Jim

No one from Black Cove was finding ship life easy . . .

(Cut to sleeping quarters.
Silent Sue and Red Ruth are fighting over their
shared bunk, Job Anderson and Grey over theirs.)

Red Ruth

Silent Sue . . .
get out of that bunk!!!

Job Anderson

Watches is changing . . .
I done Starboard watch and now is Port Watch so . . .

Red Ruth

that is now my bunk not your bunk!

(Unseemly bunk tussle.)

Silver

No one but you, Jim girl!
You look like you was born for the sea . . .
you are a true born sailor
like
Black Cat . . .

(Cut to Black Dog, piece of fine seamanship.)

Like Kind Killigrew –

(Cut to Killigrew, ditto.)

Like Joan The Goat

(Cut to medical room.)

Joan

Aaaaaaghyevillainyeblackguardyeswabyedevilye
diggingprobingpullinghammeringhellion!!!! . . .

Dick
    Don't bleed . . . this is best Bristol Bombazine!

Doctor
    Stop screaming, Joan The Goat!
    I cannot hear myself / hammer!

    (*Cut back to galley.*)

Silver
    although not so accident-prone . . .
    a true-born sailor
    like Israel Hands

    (*Cut to Israel Hands at wheel, fine steering . . .
        Then . . . a sudden glitch, which makes everyone
    on the ship tilt.*)

    only . . . you weren't born with clumsy hands!!!!

    (*And they both laugh . . . hold up for each other's
    amusement, say a parsnip or a potato, whittled into
    say, a sailor! a ship!*)

    (*Suddenly alert to something new.*) Come with me, Jim!

    (*Jim and Silver ascend to deck . . .*)

Jim
    What is it?

Silver
    Smell that salt!
    Feel that wind!
    Something's up.
    We're best on deck.

    (*On each ship level, some small object tips over . . .
        In the galley, the peanut jar tips and . . .*)

Flint
    Pieces of eight

Pieces of eight . . .
(*Finds.*) *Peanut!*

(*Such an adorable parrot . . .*
    Silver and Jim make it on to deck . . .)

Silver
Stand here in lea of me, Girl
Storm's coming.

Captain
Batten down hatches!

Crew
Aye aye Sir!!!

(*Preparations for a great storm.*)

Silver
How I do *love* a storm!!!

FOURTEEN
STORM

Jim
My ship fought the mightiest storm!
My crew were magnificent!!!!
We were a *storm-fighting machine*!!!

(*Sailing crew run ship brilliantly . . .*)

All but my *landlubbing* friends . . .

Doctor
Below . . .
Oh this *sea*!
Oh these *waves*!
Oh dear me I must
Bleurrrghhhhhh . . .

Squire
The ship is breaking!
We will be flotsam!
We will be jetsam!
We are going to go down!!!!
We will be food for sharks!

Silver
Do your worst, winds and waves!!!!

(*Silver almost conducts the storm.*)

Squire
We're for drowning we're for *drowning*!!!

(*And a huge wave rocks the ship and Jim is pitched almost overboard . . .*
But Silver incredibly rapidly, leaps and saves her . . .)

Jim
You saved me!

Silver
What are friends for?

(*And the storm peaks!*)

FIFTEEN
STARS

Back to normal sailing as . . .

Jim
Long John . . .
The one-legged man of *my nightmare*???? (*As if!*)
No!

Squire
Dear Friend
I didn't think I could hold you in *more esteem* than
already I do . . .

But you saved this girl's *burgeoning* life.
I thank you, Sir, I thank you!!!!

Jim

There are *millions* of one-legged men on *The Sea*!
Sailing's a *Dangerous* Life!
Us *Sailors* are *ever* in peril!
Long John / is

Doctor

A Hero and Gentleman, Sir.

Jim

And
My *Best* Friend on All The *Hispaniola*!!

Silver

Shall I show you some magic, Jim?

Jim

Yes!

Silver

Around us nothing but sea.
Where we are?

Jim

I don't know!

Silver

Night's drawing in.
See anything . . .?

Jim

A *star*!

(*In the sky, a light . . .*)

Silver

A *planet*.

Venus!

(Another light . . . Jim spots . . .)

Jim

Another planet!

Silver

Star
Vega
Look . . .

(Both spot . . .)

Jim

Yellow star

Silver

Capella
And stars soon makes *shapes* . . .

Jim

Upside-down M!!!

Silver

Cassiopeia . . . but renamed *Upside-down M*
What is *that* shape . . . ?

Jim

Saucepan!

Silver

Hereafter known as *Long John's Saucepan*!!!
All these stars and shapes is *moving*, Jim . . .
Save one immoveable star
Which Long John's Saucepan will lead you to . . .

(Takes up a saucepan.)

Lift its handle like you're pouring stew . . .

(Jim does.)

See the side the stew pours out . . . ?

Jim

Yes

Silver

Now see it in the *sky* saucepan . . .

Jim

Yes
Two bright stars . . .

Silver

Yes, now put your fist between those two bright stars

(*She does.*)

Now . . . that's your measuring tool . . .

Jim

My fist?

Silver

Count how many fists up the sky and find the very
brightest star . . .

Jim

With fist . . . one two three four five . . .
Bright bright star!!!!

Silver

North Star.
Polaris.
The one constant immoveable star

Jim

Like Grandma

Silver

Named hereafter . . . '*Grandma!*'
Now for the magic . . .
We use all this to find where we are in this dark
empty sea . . .
We look to the horizon . . .

We put out our measuring fist . . . thumb flat atop . . .
Count how many fists up to Polaris . . .

Jim

Grandma
Six

Silver

And hey presto . . .you have turned into a sextant!

Jim

What's a sextant?

Silver

A sextant
is an instrument for measuring *latitude*

Jim

I'm a human instrument for measuring latitude!!!

(*How cool is that?*)

What's latitude?

Silver

Your distance northwards or southwards
from the equator
so
human sextant . . .
how many fists from horizon to Grandma's star?

Jim

Six

Silver

if each fist is ten degrees . . .
six be

Jim

sixty degrees

Silver

And that's your latitude . . .

And that's where you are right now!
Latitude sixty degrees!

Jim
I know exactly where I am on this deep dark sea!

Silver
I cannot make out a single line of writing . . .
but I can read the whole *book* of stars!

Jim
I can now read both words and stars!

Silver
You can now   find your way safe through all this evil
    world.
Abracadabra!!!

SIXTEEN
AN APPLE BARREL

Jim heads for the apple barrel . . .

Jim
Everyone was in the bravest spirits
That night
We should sight our Treasure Island . . .

Grey (*on deck*)
Look!
Albatross!
Can anybody else see it?
Can anybody hear me?
Grey here?

(*But no one can.*)

Jim
For *once* I *should like* one of the Doctor's apples.

(Goes to the apple barrel . . .)

There was still some in the very bottom of the . . .

(Reaches in . . .
    Falls into it . . .
    From inside the barrel . . .
    She moves apples . . . finds . . .)

THE MAP!!!!
Oh Clever Doctor!

(Silver, Parrot, Black Dog, Killigrew, Joan, Dick,
Badger and Hands burst in around it . . .)

Silver
Dog!
Bring that barrel!
Map's nowhere to be found!
That *CabinGirl* ain't coughing its location!
Time for Mathematics, Mutineers!

(Joan the Goat, Dick and Killigrew manhandle in Job
Anderson, Red Ruth, Silent Sue and Lucky Micky.
Ram Job against the barrel. Hold him either side . . .)

Explain the Maths, Black Dog.

Black Dog
Well, *Landlubber . . .?*
You going to join along of us . . .

Job Anderson
I'm not joining a *mutiny*, Black Cat!

Black Dog
Black *Dog!*

Jim
Black *Dog?*

Black Dog
Join or *Swim*, Ploughman?

85

Job Anderson
    I can't *Swim and* I won't *Join*
    Damn your black heart!

Silver
    Drown him!

Job Anderson
    Not the sea not the sea!!!

    (*Silver points to . . .*)

Black Dog
    No, not the sea . . .
    Swim in this!!!

    (*They take him, hold him over a barrel of brandy . . .*)

Job Anderson
    Not *brandy*!
    I swore to *lemonade*!
    I swore to my Old Lady I wouldn't take / strong
        spirits . . .

    (*But they dunk him. He drowns, disappointing his
    wife in two ways . . .
        Silent Sue does a silent scream.*)

Badger
    I do *love* a quiet woman!!!

Joan
    One less *agin* us, Silver.

Silver
    Then, get *another* . . .

Jim
    Oh . . . who *next*????

Killigrew
    Get the Pie Eater!

Jim
Red Ruth!

Red Ruth
No!
I think it weren't *me* as ate that last pie!

Badger
I think it *were*!

Black Dog
We're for *gold* not *pie*, Peasant!
Gold!

Hands
Gold!

Dick
With us, or *against* us?

Red Ruth
Squire's been good to me . . .

Black Dog
With us or *against* us?

Silver
Against us . . . Captain Flint here will peck out yer
    eyes . . .
Right, Captain Flint . . .???

Flint
Pieces of *eight*
Pieces of *eight*

Black Dog
Eyes and Pies with *us* . . . or *No Eyes No Pies*
    with *Them?*

Red Ruth
Eyes and Pies!
With!

Black Dog
Sit down there along of us.

Silver
Next!

(They bring Lucky Micky. Hold his eyes near Parrot's beak . . .)

Black Dog
Lucky Micky
Or *Unlucky* Micky?

Lucky Micky
Lucky Micky!!!

Black Dog
Sit down along of us.

Silver
Get the Non-Blabber!

(They get Silent Sue. Stand her.)

Black Dog
With us or against us?
Give us a sign.

(Silent Sue puts two thumbs up.)

She's in!

(She's lying . . . We will discover this later . . .)

Silver
Three . . .
There's less on their side of the equation and
    more on *our* side
Odds is turning to evens
How I do *love* the pleasure of *pure* mathematics.
This deserves *grog*!!!

(Low cheering . . .)

88

Red Ruth (*terror comfort-eating*)
Any biscuit with that . . . ?

Silver
We are all that's left alive of the *Walrus* crew, my
new friend . . .
This Treasure that *Fatty* Trelawney and
Doctor *Liverish* think is *theirs*
Is rightfully and fairly *ours*

(*All agree variously . . .*)

We've lost *legs fingers brains eyes*

(*Nods of assent and fingers etc. lifted . . .
Joan headbutts the apple butt . . .
Jim and barrel lurch . . .*)

Jim
You broke Grandma's chair!!!

Silver
We Followed Squire Posh to Bristol
I find you all gainful employment so

Dick
The crew of the *Walrus*
Become –

All
The crew of the *Hispaniola*!!!

(*Roar of laughter.*)

Silver
Thanks to who?

Dick
Thanks *to you*, John Silver!!

Silver
We are now *the majority* . . .
We near the island . . .

(*All quiet and scared . . .*)

Badger
Where our six shipmates vanished so *strangely* . . .

Dick
And now do seem to

Joan
Walk in our heads dush dush dush . . .

Killigrew
Like *ghosts* . . .

Hands
Ghosts!!!!

(*Some moaning and suffering . . .*)

Silver
Which is as *nothing* to who walks my head always!!!

Black Dog
Flint!!!

Silver
Flint my *captain*!
Who I killed in his *bed*.
For why?

Badger
For treasure, Silver.

Silver
For treasure for *who*?

Black Dog
For *us*, Long John.

Silver
For you I endure in dark nights in the corner of my
    bedroom . . .
Our dead captain . . . watching me . . .

(*All very frightened . . . but . . .*)

We are very near to grasping Flint's Fist . . .
We tread careful
At the first sight of that *map*
We –

Joan
Dush!

Hands
Ó
Passer cerol
Fazer picadinho
Passer a faca
Acabar com ele
Degolar
Esquartejar   apunhalar   tirar as tripas.

Silver
Israel Hands, . . . speak *soft*, work *nice*
Till I give the word

Hands
Yes, Long John Silver!

Badger
But *when*?

Silver
The last moment I can manage is *when*.
When I has the map in one hand *a spade* in my other
And the island beneath my feet . . .
I've set foot already on that island, I know it *well*!
So . . . We subtract and smile until
We shake hands at last with
Flint's Fist . . .

(*Glasses raised . . .*
    All sing 'Fifteen men on a dead man's chest'.)

Silver
Perhaps . . .

(*It takes a while but . . .*)

Grey
Dick . . .
You must jump up, like a sweet lad,
And get me one of spindly-girlboy's apples to wet my
  pipe like . . .

(*And as Dick's hand reaches in the barrel and almost
touches Jim's face . . .*)

Grey Land ho!

(*Crew all rush to look as . . .*)

SEVENTEEN
OFFSHORE

*Jim crawls out of the barrel holding the map . . .
  On deck . . .*

Captain
Rig capstan
Weigh anchor!

Crew
Aye aye, Captain!!!!

(*And sing . . . as ship is anchored and dismantled . . .
  Jim holds an apple in one hand, the map in the
other.*)

Jim
My crew had sailed the sea.
My ship had reached its destination.
My anchor was weighed.
We were in shallow calm water.

Here the map
Just *there*
The island with its treasure . . .
And inside me
A storm more terrible than ever I met at sea . . .

(*Jim, Captain, Squire, Doctor congregate in captain's cabin . . .*)

Doctor
These are dangerous murderous men

Captain
Mutineers murderous *mutineers*!!!

Doctor
Dangerous murderous mutineers in *greater numbers* than us!
We must make *a plan* to get away from them and this island!

Captain
Assemble a reduced crew of honest men . . . sail back to England!!!

Squire
There's *treasure* there!
Almost within our grasp!!!
We came for *treasure*!

Jim
We *deserve* that treasure!

Squire
Exactly!

Jim
I *hate* Long John Silver!

Squire
I hate him *most*!
My friend!

Jim

False friend!

Captain

We must make a plan and hold it firm and fast!
We must be united!
Who is in favour of treasure?

(*Squire and Jim immediately . . . then Captain.*)

Who *against?*

(*Doctor raises hand.*)

We must secure the map somewhere safe
Who's to keep it?

Jim

Silver thinks *I* am his *friend*
The map is safest with *me*, Doctor

Doctor

I promised your Grandma I'd keep you safe!

Jim (*snatching the map*)

Give me the damn map!
I'm a *girl*, not a *baby*!!!

(*Map is back with Jim . . .*)

Captain

We need to know who is on our side

Squire (*starts counting*)

We four
And all my people
Silent Sue
Job Anderson
Red Ruth
Lucky Micky . . .

Jim

Not Red Ruth not Lucky Micky . . .

Silver   and his *parrot* was most persuasive with them.
Silent Sue . . . I could not see if she did thumbs up or
    thumbs down . . .

(*Sad mime of two thumbs straight up.*)

Squire
    I am *heartbroken*!

Doctor
    We must try to get them back!

Squire
    You are always in the right
    Try to get them back!

Captain
    We must lower a jolly boat . . .
    Those loyal to us must stay on the ship . . .
    Those disloyal
    In the jolly boat . . .
    They will to the island
    Where we will *strand* and *starve* them into surrender.

Squire
    Yes, get them in the jolly boat and
    Jolly well *strand* them
    And they can jolly well *starve*

Doctor
    How do we do this, Captain?

Captain
    Like gentlemen and sailors, Doctor . . .

    (*And they make their way on deck . . .*)

With the clear eyes of truth
The proud hearts of courage
And the sharp swords of righteousness ready in our
    scabbards!

EIGHTEEN
JOLLY JOLLY BOATS

Deck . . .
Crew assembled . . .

Captain (*sotto voce to goodies*)
I will seem to chose men randomly . . .

Silver (*sotto voce to baddies*)
I want some o' you swabs shipside . . .
some of you shoreside . . .

Captain
Men
We have come through rough seas and storm
But we have our island in our sight
Our treasure lies waiting
We are lowering jolly boats to take you ashore

Jim
First jolly boat ready, Captain!

Captain
Six places in the jolly boat!
Who first to get their land legs back?

(*Red Ruth / Grey / Dick / Killigrew / Black Dog / Joan / Lucky Micky / Silent Sue / Squire / Doctor all put their hands up.*)

Captain
Most deserving . . . I think . . .
Killigrew . . . Dick . . . Goat . . .

Squire (*acting*)
Not I, Captain????

Captain
Not you, Squire.

Squire
Damme I'm disappointed.

Captain
Three places taken!
Who next to get walk about on solid ground?

(*Black Dog / Badger / Squire / Doctor / Red Ruth /
Silent Sue / Lucky Micky / Grey put their hands up.*)

Squire / Doctor (*acting*)
Me, Captain!!!!
I, sir!!!!
Please, Captain!!!!

Captain
But six places in the jolly boat, Lads!

Badger
He won't pick me!
Captain hates me!
It's not *fair*.

Captain
Black Dog
Red Ruth.

Squire
Ah, Red Ruth! . . . Lucky Micky! . . . disappointed like
    Your Squire!
Silent Sue!
Thumbs up . . . with me????

(*Silent Sue does thumbs up.*)

Grey
I'll go in the first jolly boat, shall I?
See my hand up?
No?

Captain
But one place left in the jolly boat!

97

Jim (*acting*)
Silver should go take last place in the jolly boat!
He has worked hardest all voyage

Doctor
Yes!
I vote Silver for last place!

Squire

I too!
Long John . . . you might like to get your land legs
back!

Silver
Land *leg*, Sir . . . hardly worth it!
Jim, *you* step in the boat . . .
This looks a sweet spot to get ashore on
Ah, to be young and have ten toes to set on firm land!

Jim
Silver, *you* step into the boat with your *five* toes
After all, *you've* been there before!

(*Silver and mutineers go very still . . .*)

Silver
Now, how could you know *that*?

(*Beat.*)

Jim
You told me.

Silver
I did not.
I told only my old shipmates.

(*Beat.*)

Walrus crew, we are *uncovered*
Take the ship!

(*And dangerous weapons out . . .*)

Captain
Hispaniola crew
Save the ship!

(*And a most dangerous fight . . . in which . . .
Silver tries to get the map from the Squire . . .*)

Silver (*with a sword at Squire's throat*)
The map, Squire!

Squire (*parrying*)
Don't have it, Swine!

(*Black Dog tries to get map from Jim.*)

Black Dog
I can smell treasure map on you!!!

Jim
And I can smell villainy on you!

(*Slash . . .*)

I *knew* you smelled familiar!

(*Parry.*)

You're Black Dog, you *Dog*!

Black Dog
And a very rare fighting very killing breed too, my pet!

(*Bares teeth . . . barks and thrusts . . .*)

Arfarfarf!!!

(*Killigrew stalks Silent Sue.*)

Killigrew
Map, Miss . . .
Into my hands!!!

(*She is on his back, he cannot reach her . . .
Badger chasing Grey.*)

Badger

Why do I get to fight the one I can't ever remember
where he is!
It's not fair!

(*Throws a marlinspike at Grey, who is somewhere
else.*
Silver now fighting Doctor for map.)

Silver

The map must be with you, Doctor!

Doctor

No map, Villain!

Silver

I'll painfully remove your *hands*

Doctor

I'll surgically remove your *head*!

(*Squire and Red Ruth fighting . . .*)

Red Ruth

Map! Squire!

Squire

Lay down your *sword*, you are attacking your *Squire*.

Red Ruth

Silver said if I didn't go with him,
He'd remove my *eyes* so I couldn't see *pies*, Squire!

Squire

Red Ruth, if you don't come with *me* . . .
No more pies! *Ever!!*

Red Ruth

Never?

Squire

Ever!

Red Ruth

I'll come back to *you*, Squire!!!

(*They stand side by side.*)

Both En garde!

(*And into the fray!*
Silver sneaks up on Jim.
She turns just in time . . .)

Jim

I thought you might come like a coward!

Silver

Like someone who's smart as paint!
Dear friend . . .
I think it might be *your* pretty fist that holds the map.

Jim

And you'd have to cut it from my *arm* before it would
     hand it to *you*
False Foe!

(*And they fight on as . . .*
Doctor and Lucky Micky fighting . . .)

Doctor

Lucky Micky . . .
I brought you *into* this world!
Why would you throw in your lot with these dark
     villains????

Lucky Micky

Since this whole bagatelle began . . .
I been on such a streak of luck . . .
I find a *groat* in a *cowpat*
Then a fine *cosh* on a quay . . .
Then a flying fish flap! At my feet!
Now twinkling treasure almost in my fingers!
A man follows his *luck*!

Apologies, Doctor but . . .

(*And he tries to sink his blade into the Doctor, who
    dodges . . .
    Jim has Silver with her sword at his throat.
    She has the map.*)

Jim
Surrender, Long John Silver!
I have you and the map!

Silver
Well, she had the map all along . . .
What d'you think of *that*, Captain Flint????

(*Parrot swoops.*)

Flint
Pieces of eight
Pieces of eight
Pieces of eight!

(*Seizes the map . . . Flies about . . .*)

Doctor
The parrot's got the map!

Jim
Captain Flint!
Bad parrot evil parrot!!!

(*Mayhem.*)

Doctor
Get the map!
Jim!
The parrot is in the rigging
Climb, girl!
Do *not* lose that map!!!

Jim (*climbs*)
Captain Flint . . .

Flint
   Nackleass

Jim
   Give me the map . . .

Flint
   Fartleberry!

Jim
   Nice parrot pretty parrot . . .
   Give me the map . . .

Flint
   Pieces of eight

Jim
   Pieces of apple . . . ?????

Silver
   Shoot the girl!

   (*All mutineers aim their pistols . . . Then it all goes to black . . .*
      Jolly Roger appears . . .)

End of Act One.

Act Two

ONE
THE ISLAND

The island of Billy Bones' horrors, shaped and smelling like a dead man's corpse . . . Hot, bright and steamy . . . The land has a strange unnerving language . . . Insects buzz and bite . . . There are odd bumps and shapes . . . One of the odd bumps suddenly sits up. It is Ben Gunn, cabin boy, but we do not know this yet . . . He has heard something odd . . . He's going to take a careful look. This is the first time in three years Ben Gunn has spoken out loud . . .

Ben Gunn (*trying to breathe in useful amounts of bad island air*) Ip ip   ip   ip   ip!

Urg urg urg   urg . . .

(*Because he has seen . . .*)

Shi shi shi shi shi shi . . . (*He is trying to say 'ship'.*)

Whaaaaaaaaaaaa . . .? (*He is trying to say 'What ship exactly?'*)

Waaaaaaaaaaaaaaaa   llllllllllllll   rrrrrrrrrrr ussssssss?????? (*'Is it . . . gulp, the Walrus?????'*)

Wiiiiiiiii . . . thhhhhhhh . . . Sssssssssssssssssssssssssssss . . . (*Dares not say 'Silver'.*)

One-lllllllllllllllllllllllll . . . (*Dares not say 'leg'.*)

Oh baaaaaaaaaaaaaaaaaaaaaaa . . . dddddddi fffffrie . . . (*Almost too upset to say 'bad friend'.*)

Down the Chi   mmmmm   leyyyyyyyyyyyy!!!!!

(*And disappears down a hole.*)

Under the unrelenting sun . . .
    Manacled and chained . . . Captain, Squire, Doctor,
Red Ruth, Grey and Silent Sue . . .
    At a distance, a pile of grog, vittles, powder, shot,
tobacco . . . The Doctor's medical bag etc. . . .
    Guarding them . . . weaponed and threatening . . .
Dick the Dandy, Killigrew, Black Dog, Joan the Goat,
Badger and Lucky Micky . . . all are very uneasy and
scared . . .
    Silver pacing back and forth . . .
    The island is whispering and murmuring . . .

Silver
    Captain Flint . . .????
    Damme . . . it that *you a-murmuring to me . . .*?

Joan
    Allardyce . . .?
    O'Doherty . . .
    Giant Grimes . . . is that you?

Dick
    Ghosts . . . I can sense them . . .

Black Dog
    I can smell 'em!
    I can feel 'em in my bones!

Silver
    Damme, *silence with your ghosts!!!!*

    (*But looks around terrified nonetheless . . .*)

    Let us work on wretched humanity instead . . .

    (*Before Squire.*) Your *wretched slithery spindly* cabin
        girl
    Is *somewhere* on this steaming pile of *island* . . .

Dripping wet and alone on the *one hand* –

(*As, with one hand, he hits Squire about the head.*)

but *free* and *treasure-mapped* on *the other hand* –

(*As, with his other hand, he hits the Doctor about the head.*)

Cosh, Lucky Micky!!!

(*Lucky Micky hands over his lucky cosh . . .*)

So *gentlefolk . . .*
One More Time . . .

(*He coshes Captain across his head . . . hands back cosh . . .*)

Recite me all the coordinates of the treasure map!!!!!

Captain
Mutineer
ONE MORE TIME
I never *saw* the map
I *said* from the *beginning* of this *bloodstained*
    foolishness I *detest* and *abhor* 'treasure'
I am thus far proved *Seer* and *Prophet*
Box about, *Blaggard*, I tell you *nothing*!!!

(*Silver raises his fist to Squire.*
    Black Dog growls menacingly . . .)

Silver
Coordinates, Sir Squire!

Squire
I have *forever* lost my faith in English men and
    women!
This *heartbreak* has driven all coordinates from my
    head!
I have *nothing* in my brain!
Box and Bite away!

Silver

I *believe* you have *nothing* in your brain, Squire *Stupid*!

(*So Silver puts a dagger to Doctor's throat . . .*)

But our clever doctor does have a brain and will
   remember the coordinates I'm sure . . .

Doctor

I am *miserable*!
I *promised* that orphan child's grandmother on my
   honour
I would *Look after her*!
I made that *wretched* map more important to me
Than a *child*
I let her fall into the terrible sea!
For what?
For *treasure*!!!
I am *beneath contempt*!
End me!
Push in your dagger . . . *push in!*!!!

Silver

How I *loathe goody-good* people with their remorse
   and morals and *honour* and patriotism nonsense . . .
(*Super sweet.*) Red Ruth, dear woman . . .
Map coordinates . . .?

Red Ruth

My stomach thinks my throat's been cut . . .
You *know* I can't *think* when I'm hungry, Barbecue . . .

(*Dick the Dandy hits her across the head . . .*)

Dick

We know you can't think *ever, Land Pig*!!!

(*Joan the Goat seizes Silent Sue and shakes her as . . .*)

Joan

Tell us the blaggardingbloodybelaying *coordinates*
   Silent Scream / tell us the *coordinates* . . .

Black Dog
Goat . . . goat . . . *GOAT!!!*

Joan
What *what*????

Black Dog
That 'un can't *speak.*

Joan
DammmeBlastZoundsDrattation!!!!

Black Dog (*seizes Grey*)
Try This 'un!!!

(*They shake vigorously . . . rough him up a bit as . . .*)

Grey
Grey!
Nice to be noticed, thank you, Sirs, but
Nobody ever remembered to show *me* the map . . .

Silver
Lying!
Liars!
As a simple *honest* cook . . .
Lying leaves a *very nasty* taste in my mouth . . .
A very nasty taste
Remove their wigs!

(*Wigs knocked off, thrown aside . . .*)

Here's the recipe for *today*, rogues . . .
Let them *sun dry*
Let them smoke let them *kipper* . . .
Let their brains *cook to a light bake* . . .
Killigrew, Dog . . .
You *remain* a-guarding . . . turn 'em occasional so they
    get an *even* browning

(*Pirates laugh . . .*)

Goat, Badger, Dick, let's you and me be off *a-foraging*
For Barbecue's recipe to *work*
We need a few pounds of fresh juicy *girl* flesh to *fry up.*
And *THE MAP*
With its list of *vital ingredients*!!!

(*Silver exits with Goat, Dick, Lucky Micky and
Badger, as . . .*)

Badger
That's *my* cosh!

Lucky Micky
My cosh.

Badger
It's not fair!

(*Black Dog and Killigrew remain, keen to bite and
throttle . . .*)

Black Dog
Grrrrrr . . . rfff!!!

Killigrew
My *stranglers* is waiting!

Black Dog
Bake like the Cornfed Chickens ye are!!!

Killigrew
Fry like the Field Fowl ye are!!!

Dog / Killigrew (*fun threatening*)
Grrrr! . . . wuff! . . .

(*Joke throttling . . .*
   *Dog and Killigrew laugh heartily. God, they're
witty!*
   Laughter dies, as they realise resentfully . . .)

Killigrew

Truth . . .?
I'm frying here *too*, Dog

Black Dog

Truth . . .?
I'm *baking* here too, Killigrew!

Killigrew

My very *throttlers* is sweatin'!!!

Black Dog

Sun's taking all my bark and spittle!
I'm getting up a rare mighty thirst here, Killigrew!!!!

Killigrew

Truth, Dog!

(*Beat.*
    *They feel very sorry for themselves. Pirate life is
sooo hard . . .*)

Dog . . .

(*Black Dog looks enquiringly . . .
    Killigrew indicates . . .*)

Grog.

Black Dog

Rrrrruffffff!!!

(*They move towards the grog/vittles/powder/shot pile
    as . . .*)

THREE
WET JIM MEETS THE MONSTER

*Another part of the island . . .
    Jim drops from somewhere hidden . . .
    She is dripping wet, exhausted and in a very bad mood.*

Jim

What a long swim!

What very *difficult* and *unhelpful* tides round this
island!

I am most *sticky* with salt from swimming ashore
and . . .   Father's breeches are chafing me very
sorely!

(*Looks around.*)

I hate Billy Bones' island! I do swear it *listens*
I hate its heat, *its black hair*, *its indigestion*!

(*Island belches.*)

Its *Bad Breath!*

(*Steps in something soft.*)

Its Flabby Flesh!
Most of all . . . *its conversation*!!!

(*Island enunciates . . .*)

Its clicking and buzzing and (*worst of all*) *glooping* . . .

(*Clicking, buzzing and glooping . . .*)

(*Very upset.*) I do not know what has happened to my
friends . . .
(*Possibly, terribly.*) Captured . . .?
(*Possibly worse.*) Dead???
(*Don't think about it!*) At least I saved *the map*!!!

(*Opens it out as . . .*)

Perhaps it will tell me which direction to . . .

(*Beat.*)

*She lifts up the map. There is a large bullet-shaped hole
in its centre.*

Damme Sharp-Shooting Madging Fartleberry Pirates!!!

(*A sudden strange glooping.*)

Something's . . . glooping!!!!!

(*Something is glooping!!!*)

Oh . . . Grandma!!!!

(*She approaches the glooping . . . A strange swamplike creature pops up from the ground in front of her . . .*)

Aaaagh!!!

Ben Gunn
Aaagh!!!!

They stare at each other in unabashed horror.

Jim
What are You????

Ben Gunn
Ip ip ip ip

Jim
Are you *human???????*

Ben Gunn
Nnnnn   sh . . . (*Not sure any more.*)
I'm Ben Gunn I haven't spoken to any one but myself these past three years THREE YEARS!!!!! haven't you Ben Gunn????
What Ben Gunn SPEAKUP!!!!! Spoken to anyone but yourself these past three years? No NO!!!!! I haven't so you're . . . Ben Gunn????
I am are you yes I am YES I AM!!!!

(*Stares more.*)

What are you????

(*Nips her.*)

Jim
Ouch NO!!!! Why did you nip me?

Ben Gunn

See if you is real or product of my probably now
diseased brain!

Jim

Yes I is real!!!!

Ben Gunn

Mightn't have a bit of cheese about you?

(*Ben searches Jim for cheese . . .*)

Jim

Don't do that

Ben Gunn

I haven't had cheese not real cheese for three years

Jim

I'm serious don't do that

Ben Gunn

I've had cheese of the diseased imagination but it's not
the same   as real cheese

(*Jim tries to unclamp Ben Gunn's searching hands . . .*)

Real *Toasted* cheese

Jim

Stop searching me Ben Gunn or / I will

Ben Gunn

That ship out there . . . Is that a real ship if so what
ship name quick name quick name quick!!!!

(*Nips her.*)

Jim

Why don't you swim out and nip it . . . find out for
yourself????

Ben Gunn

Ben Gunn can't swim.

Ben Gunn has dreamed of a real ship almost more
than he's dreamed of cheese.

Ben Gunn wishes he could get on that ship and sail
HOME don't you Ben Gunn?

Oh yes to a SAFE WARM PLACE with more than
ME some GOOD humans and Real CHEESE
TOASTED for PREFERENCE!!!!

Is that your ship?

Jim

Yes!

Ben Gunn

Wwwwwwwwwwwwwwwwwwwone-llllllegged
man on it at all??????

Jim

Yes!

Ben Gunn

Ssssssssssssssssssssssssil   vvvvvvvvvvver . . . ???????

Jim

Yes!

You know Long John Silver????

Ben Gunn

Ip   ip

*(In immense dread, Ben Gunn loses power of
breathing.)*

Jim

How do you know Long John Silver???
How????
Speak!

Ben Gunn

Ip

Jim

You're soooo thin . . . !!!! scrawny almost . . . you're
the cabin boy the scrawny cabin boy!!!!!

Ben Gunn

Ip   ip ip

Jim

Just nod

(*Ben Gunn nods.*)

On the *Walrus*!!!????
Just nod!

(*Ben Gunn nods.*)

They left you on the island?

(*Nods.*)

Why?
Were you bad?
Did they just forget you?
I'm a Pirate-Fighter you need to tell me . . .

(*Ben Gunn can't speak.*)

Ben Gunn if you can get some words out . . . I'll put
you on my ship
And feed you cheese . . .

(*Brilliant fact-getting strategy! It releases . . .*)

Ben Gunn

Silver says CaptainFlintwants sixreliableswabstobury
yourtreasureonthisherehandyisland.
He says I picked already
AllardyceO'DohertyMcGrawThimbleGiantGrimes
Who for the sixth?
Silver says 'Captain Flint, take Ben Gunn along of you
forheistheonlywritingPersononboardship sohecan

write thecluesfortherefinding oftreasureandheis
smart as paint.'

Jim

He said that to *me*!

Ben Gunn

And looked out for *you too*?

Jim

Right up until the time he *didn't*

Ben Gunn

Right up until the time he *didn't*!!!!

Jim

Which was?

Ben Gunn

My firstdayonthismadmakingisland!!!
Ip
Ip
Ip

Jim

Tell me

Ben Gunn

Silverrowsusshiptoisland
'A one-leggedmanain'tnouseinburyingtreasure . . .
I'llwaithereinthejollyboat
Takeyouislandtoship' hesaysand
we six and Flint find a SWEET spot we six start
    diggging

(*His breath labours with fear.*)

Ip ip ip ip

Jim

What ?

Ben Gunn

Hole's very deep   ip
Sun's very hot   ip
Other five is in the hole hole's deepening   ip
I'm writing down cluesinrhyme!!! I finish says to
    Captain I've done the clue sir in verse, Sir . . .
Ip   ip
Flint says Cabin boy go fill my flask with water from
    that pool . . .
I go   I come back

(*He's stopped breathing in dread He mimes to Jim . . .
'Nip me'. Jim nips him as . . .*)

Jim

You came back . . . what?   Nip, harder nip . . . fact-
    releasing nip . . .

Ben Gunn

ThefiveisshottheirtheirHEADSEVERYONE!!
    andCaptainFlintis just thenreloadinghissmoking
    pistolstomakemedeadwith HOLEINHEAD
    NUMBER SIX!!!!
Ip   Ip   Ip

Jim

But he didn't make you number six!
Why?

Ben Gunn

Flint says . . . now Boy . . .
You're powerful scrawnyIdon'twantmypistolballto
    whistlepastyou comeverynearerhereso'sI canPLUG
    YOUPAINLESSLY . . . .
But my feets won't go *forward*
They insist on a going *backward*
And . . . I

(*He falls down a hole.*)

Jim

Where are you????

Ben Gunn (*from within hole*)

I fall down a hole and I'm in tunnels . . . I noticed you
noticed   I'm still on the scrawny side?

(*Jim nods politely.*)

I feelSAFEin tunnelsscrawninessisaGIFTintunnels
Ithink Ben Gunn runrunrun
I'll tell my Best Friend Silver He'll save me from Flint.
I tunnels up jolly boat vicinity see him sitting . . .
I opens my mouth to say 'friend Silver, help'
And I hears Him say
Ip Ip Ip
'Ho Flint . . . did ye show them all the mathematics of
taking away six and leaving one?' No says Flint,
I'm one short that scrawn he disappeared into thin
air and my friend my friend my friend says . . .
'We *got to pop* that one too . . .'
We got *to subtract* him from the equation . . . he's
smart as paint!!'

Jim

Knackleass!!

Ben Gunn

Tide's turning says Flint He won't last a week without
me feeding   'im stew says my BADBADBADBAD
FRIEND . . . And if he survives I'll kill 'im with
MYVERYOWNHANDS when we return to up dig
That treasure!!!!and now he's returned to up dig
that treasure and kill me WITHHISVERYOWN
HANDS ip   ip   ip   ip!!!!!!!

(*He's now uber-uber-terrified . . .*)

Jim

Ben Gunn. I *swear* on a lump of the *tastiest* cheese
I will be your true friend

We are both smart as paint, with four legs between
    us and *two* . . . one and *a half* good brains!
We will defy and defeat our one-legged nightmare!
    How does this reverse chimney system work?

Ben Gunn
You have to go head first

Jim
Head first into *mud*?

Ben Gunn
Just . . . *dive*!

(*And dives head first into the ground.*)

Jim
Dive!

(*And he follows Ben Gunn into the ground.*)

FOUR
STRATEGIES

The chained and manacled prisoners . . .
    Black Dog and Killigrew lying across each other . . .
both with an emptied grog bottle . . . both snoring
syncopatedly . . .
    Sun still beating down . . .

Squire
I feel like a steamed pudding!

Red Ruth
Ooo . . . I could *murder* a steamed pudding, Squire . . .
My stomach thinks my throat has been cut!

Captain
Thinking on *Puddings* will Addle our Brains more
    than this *Relentless* sun!

Look . . .
That grog-pickled pirate pair have fallen into *a stupor*
This is our chance to *escape* if we can only hatch an
    escape plan!
Belay and *Think*!!!!

(*They think . . .*
        Doctor looks at the locks.
        *Silent Sue appears to be having a lot of ideas . . . she
is trying every position . . .*)

Doctor
The locks on these *infernal* manacles are of a simple
    rudimentary
Construction . . .
If only I could reach my *medical* bag . . .
There are instruments in there which we could
Employ as *lock picks* . . .

Captain
Let's try to *inch* our way *thatwards* . . .

Squire
Or *thiswards* . . .

(*They try . . .*)

Captain
Courage Crew!

Squire
Pull!!!

Captain
Heave!
Haul out the cat!
Rig capstan!

(*They form themselves, at the Captain's command,
into a variety of ship-shapes but . . .*)

Doctor
Hopeless!

Red Ruth
They have hammered a *marlinspike* into the damned
  rock!!!
We are pinned *here*!!!

(*They try a whispered rendition of 'Haul away, Joe'. It
doesn't help . . .
  They strain to no avail . . .*)

Doctor
If *only* there was a way to reach my *damned bag*!!!

(*Grey quietly gets up.
  Goes and gets the bag.
  He is unmanacled . . .*)

Captain
What the *tarnation*???

Squire
Who the *devil* is that????

(*Grey hands the bag to the Doctor.*)

Grey
Grey, Sir.
Saw the albatross . . .?
Nobody remembers me . . .
Even when it comes to chaining me up.

(*Opens Doctor's bag . . .*)

What can I hand you, Doctor . . .?

Doctor
Scalpel . . .

Grey
Grey . . . Scalpel . . .

(*Doctor fiddles with scalpel . . .*)

Doctor
Hopeless!
Forceps please . . .

Grey
Forceps . . . *Grey.*

(*Passes forceps . . .*)

Flint (*off*)
Pieces of eight
Pieces of eight
Where's the pieces of eight?

Captain
Silver and his mutineers returning!

Squire
Speedier, Doctor . . .

Doctor
Damnation!
Pistol, Grey!

Grey (*handing double-barrelled pistol*)
Pistol, Doctor . . .

(*Doctor shoots two locks off . . .*
Others look mystified . . .)

Squire
Pistol, Doctor?

Doctor
Just *sometimes* my patients require me to put a quick
merciful and pain-free end to them!

Captain
Quick . . .
Unchain
Unlock

Relieve these varmints of the powder the shot the
    vittles and cetera . . .

(*Squire seizes brandy, goes to swallow, as Red Ruth
stuffs an entire pie in her mouth.*)

Squire
    I'm so thirsty!

Red Ruth
    My stomach thinks my throat's been cut!!!

Doctor
    Not *brandy* Squire!

Captain
    Legs to work, not *jaws*!
    Belay and Beat a Retreat!!!!

    (*Grey seizes another pistol from Killigrew's hand.
        Silent Sue seizes everything, whether useful or not . . .
        They exit over the sleeping Black Dog and Killigrew.
        Silver and pirates arrive.*)

Silver (*furious*)
    What Happened Here????

    (*He kicks Black Dog in the head
        He kicks Killigrew in the head.*)

    Little *Sleepy* were we, Lads????
    Forty Winks, Was It????

    (*He drags them to the pile of empty chains . . .*)

    Notice anything *different* about this *picture*,
        Tosspotters????

    (*Black Dog and Killigrew sway in stereo, trying to
    focus through their grog spectacles.*)

Black Dog
    World's *tipping* . . .

(*All pirates look to Silver in disappointment.*)

Badger

Well, Long John . . .
You left some wrong choices here a-guarding

Dick

Took us Traipsing through *thorn* and *thistle* in my *one*
   outfit!!!

Joan

Didn't find the *girl* didn't find the *map*
That's give me *the headache* that has!

Lucky Micky

Haven't found a thing since I set foot on this island . . .
Not a thing
It's like you're not so lucky for me sudden, Silver . . .

Flint

Where's the map?
Where's the vittles?
Where's the grog?

(*And they see the vittles and grog have gone . . .*)

Dick

Oh, that's very untidy that is!!!

(*Badger makes a leadership bid. He is eye to eye with Silver.*)

Badger

Well Silver . . .
You took *us* on a wild goose chase!

Joan

Wild *goose-girl* chase! *Dush!*

Badger

You decided to leave two tosspots
To guard *everything*.

Joan

Two known and noted Tosspots . . . *Dushdush!*

Badger

We now have *no* hostages to torture
No grog to glug *no* vittles to revitalise our sagging
    spirits . . .

Joan (*headbutts something*)
DushDushDush!!!!

Badger

This is a poor pass you've brought us to, Silver . . .
A very poor pass . . .

Flint

Where's the treasure, Knackleass????

Black Dog

Parrot's put his claw on it . . .
Where's the treasure, Silver????

Joan

Not *here* is *where*!

Dick

Perhaps we need a new leader here, Long John . . .
    eh, Badger?

Badger

Perhaps indeed . . .

Silver (*eyes holding Badger's*)
Swabs . . . you're *right*.
How could *I*, a man with but *one* leg . . .
A man of *peace* not *pistol*!
A man of *cooking* not *killing*
Lead you fine dangerous *two*-legged fellows???

(*Silver helps up Black Dog.*)

I shouldn't have left you, Dog

(*Helps up Killigrew . . .*)

I shouldn't have left *you,* Killigrew
Oh, I'm hopeless I am!
Perhaps George Badger here should be leader

(*A friendly hand on Killigrew.*)

What d'ye think, Killigrew?

Killigrew
I think *yes*

Silver
Two-legged man leading all the two-legged men

(*He has always his eye on Badger as . . .*)

Killigrew
That's how it should be!

Silver
Because . . .
Who could best George Badger?

Badger
No one

Silver
Or a great big braw Battler like you Kind Killgrew . . .?

Killigrew
No one, that's who!

Silver
No one indeed, Killigrew!

(*Puts his arm round Killigrew's shoulder's . . .
But beadily still looks at Badger.*)

How could *anyone* do *that*?

(*He is now behind Killigrew . . .*)

Unless someone come at him from *behind*!!!!

(*And, incredibly fast . . .*
　*Silver leaps on him, a knife in his hand which he
holds at Killigrew's throat . . .*
　Killigrew reaches with both hands for the knife.)

You see, even *then*, *George*, Killigrew here has the
　advantage . . .
His two big hands can wrest that knife right off Old
　Silver . . .

(*Killigrew suddenly goes rigid . . . as if receiving three
mighty blows in his back . . .*)

Unless yet again someone come at you from *behind*!!!
Like he got the *one* leg . . .
But the *two* knives!

(*Killigrew falls forward, three knife wounds in his back.*)

Whoops!
Who d'you say you wanted as leader . . . Swabs????
WHO?????

(*Beat.*
　Then . . .)

Badger
You, Long John . . .
We want *you* to be our leader!!!

Joan
I *always* wanted that!

Dick
I too!

Lucky Micky
Luckily so did I!

Silver
I'm touched by your loyalty!
Any dissent . . . George Badger . . . ?

Badger

Damned parrot *confused* me!!!
It's not fair!
I've *always* been for *you,* Silver.

Black Dog (*drunk . . . tipping*)

I've always been for . . . *both* of you!!!

Silver

What a very beautiful day it is!
What a wonderful place is this world we live in!
Are we not the luckiest Lads alive . . .?

Lucky Micky

Yes we are!

Silver

Then, let's away and look for rainbows' ends!
What do you say, Lucky Micky?

Lucky Micky

Yes, rainbows' ends, Silver!

Silver

What do we always find at rainbows' ends, Lucky
Micky . . .????

Lucky Micky

A crock of gold

Silver

Right response!
Tramp!!!

(*And . . .*)

FIVE
UNDER A BRITISH FLAG

*Grey holding Doctor's bag open . . . Doctor jabbing
various instruments here and there in the ground . . .*

Squire is smoking, watching Red Ruth searching
through some of the recaptured provisions . . .
Silent Sue is laying out something that looks
suspiciously like a picnic . . .

Doctor
If only SquireSuddenlyThirsty! had seized the water
  not the brandy!!!
Yes!
Water here!
Force-feeding tube . . .

Grey
Grey . . . force-feeding tube, Doctor . . .

(*And hands it to Doctor to draw up drinking water*
as . . .)

Squire
Keep looking, Red Ruth!
I saw it packed with my own sharp eyes!
It is in there somewhere!
It is exactly what we need now . . .
We have powder shot food grog tobacco!!!
We lack only what is in there somewhere . . .

(*Some glooping . . .*
    They all train their weapons on . . .
    Emerging . . .
    Jim and Ben Gunn.)

Jim / Ben Gunn
Don'tshootdon'tshootfriendfriend friend!!!

Doctor
. . . Jim . . . ????
Is that indeed you Jim ?????

Jim
Yes!

Squire
With the map????

Doctor
Who *cares* about / the wretched *map*, Squire??? . . .

Jim (*reveals*)
With the map, Squire!

(*Hands map to Doctor.*)

With a little bullet hole in it, Doctor . . . but . . .

Ben Gunn
Strangerswithpistolsandmusketswithprobablybullets
    inthem!!!!
BenGunnhopestheyareproductsofhislonely
    terrifiedimagination . . .

(*Ben Gunn nips Captain.*)

Captain
Ouch!
Belay!!

(*Hits Ben Gunn a backhander.*)

Ben Gunn
Owwww!!! Real Captain!

Jim
This / is

Ben Gunn
BenGunncabinboyandmerelyreluctantformerpirate!!!
    that'saREALcaptainthensomusketsandriflesare
    probablyrealtoowithrealbullets ip   ip   ip

Jim
Cabin boy on the *Walrus*!

Squire
The bloody *Walrus*!

Ben Gunn
Ben Gunn's sorry

Jim
Burier of The Treasure!

Ben Gunn
Ben Gunn's really sorry

Doctor
Intimate of the island these past three years . . .

Jim
And . . . .
The tunnels *below* the island . . . the *whole* island . . .

Ben Gunn
Veryathomewithtunnelsratherprefersthemtomuskets
pistolset. Trulysorry!!!

Red Ruth
Here it is, Squire!!!

(*She holds up a big English flag . . .*)

Squire
Then *hoist* it, Red Ruth!
We have a map!
We are after *treasure*!!
Secure the flag to that high spot up there . . .
We will show all villains what honest Englishmen and
    women
Are made of!!!

(*And Red Ruth begins to climb.*)

Doctor
Oh God *no*!!! . . .

Captain
Oh Squire *Idiot* . . .

Doctor

Squire . . . is that an *entirely* good idea?

Ben Gunn

Oh . . . up!!! *BENGUNNthinksthatisatrulyBADIDEA.*

Squire

We are *Englishmen*, Livesey!

Captain

And, surely, if we are *intelligent* Englishmen . . .
We do not announce our hiding place for every
    villain . . .

(*Red Ruth secures and unfurls a large English Flag
as . . .*)

Red Ruth

There we are, Squire!!!

(*A whirring sound . . .*
    Something whizzes across the space . . .
    Cutting a red slice across Red Ruth's throat . . .)

Squire . . .

(*It spouts blood . . .*)

Oh Squire . . .

(*She falls.*
(*Squire catches her.*
    Helps her to lie upon the ground as . . .
    *Captain, Doctor, Jim, Silent Sue, Grey, etc. look
around for the culprit . . .*)

Ben Gunn

BloodagainBENGUNNdoesn'twantbloodagain!!!

Squire

Red Ruth . . .

Red Ruth
Damme, I'm hungry!
My stomach thinks my throat has been cut!

Squire
Red Ruth . . .
Your throat has been cut!

Jim (*finds*)
This is Dick the Dandy's long-distance finisher!

Ben Gunn
DicktheDandyDICKTHEDANDYishereGOAT
    DOGBADGER willsoonfollow ip   ip   ip!!!

Captain
They have found us!

Red Ruth
Be I going, Doctor?

Doctor
Yes, Red Ruth.

Squire
Red Ruth, forgive me!

Red Ruth
No need, Squire!
You always fed me royally!

Squire
Ruth. Red

(*She spurts blood.*)

Bloodred Ruth . . .

Red Ruth
Thank you for all the pies and adventure . . . ooo . . .
I feels a bit . . . Squire say me a prayer . . .

Squire (*begins a prayer with . . .*)
    O Lord . . .

    (*And she dies . . .*)

Doctor
    She's gone.

Squire
    O Lord . . .

    (*Squire very upset in a manly way . . .*
        Silent Sue suddenly opens her mouth and cries
    loudly and surprisingly . . .)

Silent Sue
    Ruuuuuuuuuuuuuuuuuuuuuuuuuuuth . . .

Doctor (*helpfully*)
    There's an unexplored scientific notion . . .
    Grief
    Releases the voice

    (*Pats formerly-Silent Sobbing Sue.*)

    There there, Silent Sue . . . sometimes in sorrow . . . a
        silver lining . . .

Captain
    No fear for a hand that's been shot down in her duty,
        Sir.

Squire
    Sorry.
    Gunpowder in me eye.
    Sorry.
    Damnation!

Doctor
    Listen!

Flint (*far off*)
    Pieces of eight!
    Pieces of eight!

Captain
　Look!

　(*A white flag of truce flutters.*)

　White flag!

Silver (*calling*)
　Flag of truce!
　Cap'n Silver to former Captain Smollett . . . come to
　　make terms
　Gentleman to gentleman!

Captain
　Captain Silver???? Gentleman!
　Here's *double* promotion!

Ben Gunn
　Silver?????!!!IsthatLongJohnSilveryesthat'sLong
　　JohnSilversure-enough ThenBenGunnissurelyHOLE
　　INHEADWITH BLOOD thistimeRun!Go!Dive!!!!

　(*And dives headfirst down a hole.*)

Doctor (*whispers*)
　Jim! Hide!
　He may think you and the map still lost!
　We will play this liar at his own game!!!

　(*They hide Jim and the map somewhere unlikely and
　brilliant and far too small, as . . .*)

Silver (*off*)
　I'm a poor one-legged Captain of the men you have
　　deserted
　and I need your word of honour not to shoot me, Sir.

Captain
　You are *not* a captain, I have *not* deserted *any man
　　ever*
　But I remain a man of honour and you have my word
　　you stinking pile of Seagull Guano. Show yourself.

(Silver appears, Parrot on his shoulder . . .)

Silver

What a sweet pretty place!

Captain

Stow your *small talk* and State your *business*, Silver

Silver

Simple discussion of *mathematics*, Captain . . .
On your side you is minus yet *another*!

Squire

Red Ruth!
My *ploughwoman*!

Silver

Minus *ploughwoman* minus *musket power*
But on your *pluses*   is vittals, tobacco, grog
and

(Looks around.)

Do you have *Jim*?
Do you have *the map* also?

Doctor

We have neither the map nor Jim!

Silver

But we have scoured this island with a fine toothcomb!
There is no Jim *anywhere*!

Doctor

There is no Jim *here*!

Silver

My honest heart tells me you *lie*, Doctor
What do you think, Bird?

(Carries Parrot to sniff Jim out . . .)

Flint

Where's the knackleass?
Where's the fartleberry?

(Puts its head on one side, looks
    Puts its head on another looks . . .
    Hops forward . . .)
    Pecks . . . very near Jim . . .
    All the goodies pretend, with effort, there is no
danger to Jim . . .)

Where's the godemiche???

Silver
Where's the cabin girl and her map?

Flint
Where's the peanuts?
Where's the peanuts????

Silver
Ye grasping greedy pirate you.
Nothing for nothing, Bird!
Hear me well, *Ex*-Captain *Stuffshirt*
You have until nightfall to deliver her with map
Otherwise we will butcher you like pork

Captain
You hear me well, *Ex-Ship's Cook*!
You have until nightfall to come up one by one
    unarmed
I'll clap you all in irons and take you home to fair trial
    in England
If you won't I'll see you all to Davy Jones.
Now *Tramp* my lad. *Double quick* . . .
While you still have my word of honour
Not to put a bullet in your worthless carcase!

Silver
Then   there will be more corpse-making!

Captain
This is *Skeleton* Island, is it not?
Stalemate!

(*Silver walks off . . .*
   Stops . . .)

Silver
   Word of honour????
   Gentleman?

   (*Like a conjuror.*)

   Island Magic!!!

   (*A shot rings out.*
      Captain ricochets . . .)

   That's what I think of your words of *honour, Gentleman*!

   (*Captain puts a hand to his chest . . .*
      It comes away red with blood . . .)

   Whoops!
   Another subtraction, Squire!
   Always keep an eye on The Numbers, Squire!!!

   (*And exits*
      Captain falls.)

Captain
   Oh, I did *never* like to be on *land*!

   (*Jim, out of her hiding place . . .*
      Watches the fight go out of her grown-up friends.)

Jim
   Oh
   All was terrible . . .
   Captain said

Captain
   Am I dying, Doctor?

Jim
   Doctor said

Doctor
Yes, Captain . . . you are . . . another lost

Jim
Squire said . . .

Squire
This is all the fault of my stupid flag.
I will take the damn thing down!!!

(*And goes to do so as . . .*)

All
No, Squire! Go up there they'll pick you off!
They *know* where we are now!
Let it *fly*!!!!

Doctor
We're *surrounded*!
Hemmed in!
Confined!!!

(*Silent Sue Sobs piteously . . .*)

Squire
Red Ruth dead!
Captain . . .
Oh what a rash fool I've been!!!

Jim
There was but one solution . . .
Squire! Doctor . . . Let *me* give myself up!

Squire
No, Jim

Doctor
No, Jim.
I promised your Grandma I would look after you.
You will stay here.
We need *sleep* . . .

Squire

I can think of nothing!
My brain is as empty as my heart is full!

Doctor

If we can think of nothing else . . .
At daybreak . . .
We will take the map and parley a safe passage with
   it in return for
The wretched *wretched* treasure . . .

(*Doctor, Squire, Grey all find dejected positions
around and about . . .*)

Grey

When I saw the albatross . . .
I thought
Oh dear
Nobody noticed

Jim

We can't just give up!!!

(*But the others huddle down to sleep.*)

Captain

Jim!

Jim

Captain . . .

Captain

I have very little time left.

Jim

Oh Captain . . .

Captain

Don't be downhearted, Jim . . .
My next orders is arrived
My Destination Port   Death

My Departure Time   Imminent
Put me in my last jolly boat and
Push me out, Girl

(*Jim takes his hand . . .*)

Jim
Oh Captain!

Captain (*closes his eyes*)
Ah, there she lies . . . my last ship!

Jim
Ship

(*And realises.*)

Ship!
Why *everyone* has forgot *the ship*!!!
Captain . . . we need to swim and capture the ship . . .
Captain . . . *I HAVE A PLAN*!

(*But, the Captain has quietly died . . .*)

Dead! No! New Orders!!!

(*She backs away from the dead Captain.*)

Squire . . . we need to *move*

Squire (*in a huddle*)
Not now, Jim . . . it has been a terrible day.
Get some sleep

Jim
Doctor . . . I have an *idea*

Doctor (*in a heap*)
Tomorrow, Jim, it will wait until tomorrow . . .

Jim
Grown-ups!!!
(*To sobbing Sue.*) Stop snivelling!!!

You're all *hopeless*!!!
Yes, go on . . . snore!!!
I hope you have nightmares every one!!!

(*Takes a brace of pistols.*)

Grown-ups ! Just *Giver-uppers*!
I can count on no one but *myself*!!!

(*Powder horn.*
   Bullets.
   Stout dagger.)

I was going to get the *Hispaniola*
Bring her round the island
And get my hopeless stupid snoring friends *home*!!!!
What must be done must be done by *me alone*!!!

(*And vanishes . . .*)

SIX
A GHOST BOY BECOMES A REAL BOY AGAIN

Ben Gunn pops up! From somewhere underground . . .
   At the very farthest edge of everything . . .
   Extremely terrified . . .

Ben Gunn

Is*this*farenoughawayfromLongJohnSilverBen
   Gunn?!!!!????
No*!!!*butthisisas*faraway*asyoucangetfromhimonthis
   *island*isn't itBen Gunn!???

(*Thinks.*)

Yes!

He'lljustcomeandkillmenowwon'theBenGunnyeshewill
   nohewon'tI'dreallylikesomeCHEESE!!!

(*A thought.*)

Whywon'thekillmeNOWBenGunn?????!!!

(*A puzzle.*)

HEDOESN'TKNOWYOU'REALIVEDOESHE?????
NO!BenGunnhethinksyouare dead!!!

(*Thoughts drip one by one into his brain.*)

Dead!

(*Does ghastly deadface acting.
    Thought drip.*)

AGHOSTBOY!!!!

(*Does a bit of floaty ghost arms . . .*)

Woooo . . . !!!!!
PAYHIMBACK!!!!
Yes!How?Think!How?Rememberyouaresmartaspaint!!
Think think think think thinkthink *think*!

(*Thought drip.
    Does a croaky voice from beyond the grave.
    Beat . . . then . . .
    He is seized by a new cascading set of conflicting
thoughts.*)

Yes!No!Wait!What!WouldIt?No!Could it?
Yes!Yes?No!Brave?No!
BraveYesBen GunnTHINK!

(*Full of a wonderful plan, he dives and disappears.*)

SEVEN
AN UNWELCOME SURPRISE

Deck of the Hispaniola . . .
    Jim, wet through, tooled up, drops on to the deck . . .

Jim

The strong tide had sapped my strength
The haul up the anchor rope ached my arms and hurt
   my hands
But being back on my *Hispaniola* had my spirits
   soaring!!!

(*Starts walking . . .*)

Hands

Boa noite Jim Hawkeens. [Good evening, Jim Hawkins.]

(*Smoking a pipe, Israel Hands . . .*)

Jim

Aaagh!!!
I'd forgotten *all* about *you*, Israel Hands!!!
Israel Hands . . .
I am captain of this ship . . .
I *demand* you lash yourself to the wheel and
Help me sail this ship *round* the island . . .
To take all good men and true back to England!!!

(*Pause.*)

Hands

Que?

Jim (*picks up rope, some mimes*)

Rope . . . wheel . . . lash . . .
(*Holds out the rope, mimes*) . . . I'll tie you if you like –
I am taking this ship, Israel Hands

Hands

Hein?

Jim

I don't know / what you're saying!!!

Hands

Nao to entendendo nada.

Jim
  Sorry!!!

Hands
  Nao to entendendo nada mesmo.

Jim
  Sorry. I don't understand what you're saying.

Hands
  Assim nao da. Ta pensando que e o quez?
  Que berimbau e gaita?
  Berimbau nao e gaita nao.

Jim
  Israel Hands!!!!!

  (*Hands whips out a vicious dagger . . .*
    Which, being clumsy, shoots out of his hand to lie
  between them . . .)

Hands
  Whoops!

  (*They both look at the dagger . . .*
    Who's going to get it?)

Both Sorry!!!

  (*Both leap but . . .*
    Hands falls over something . . .
    Jim gets tangled in the rope . . .
    Both fall into a clumsy tangle . . .
    Terrible fight, tired girl versus eternally clumsy.)

Jim
  Sorry . . . sorry but . . . I'm really sorry . . . sorry . . .

  (*Finally . . . Jim is hopelessly tangled in ropes.*
    Hands, triumphant . . .)

Hands (*shows Jim his sacred medal*)
Sempre carpego esta
Medalha sagrada comigo
Da minha hãe querida
Ninguéh pode me matar
Ah! Meu cachcmbo!
Vou dar uma fumadinha.

(*Notices his pipe is unlit . . .*)

Cadê meu fosforo?!

(*Drops his match into very nearby gunpowder.*
Huge explosion . . .
Hands vaporises.
His sacred medal flutters down . . .)

Jim
Sorry!

(*Untangles from rope . . .*)

I must rescue my friends! Yesyesyesyesyes!!!
On *your own*! It's *impossible*! *You have to! I don't
know how!!!*
Yes you do! Oh you are turning into Ben Gunn
Shut Up and getonwithit!!!!!!!!!
Find your route!

(*Looks to the stars . . .*)

Venus
Vega
Yellow Capella
Lying Scoundrel's Saucepan
Grandma Polaris!!!!
Latitude . . . ?

(*Does sextant work?*)

One, two, three, forty   I am at forty degrees
My friends   there   which is at forty-five degrees

(And becomes her own sextant.
 Checks wind direction.)

Wind direction!
South South West!
To work!
Hoist the staysail!

(She cuts the anchor rope . . .)

Cast off!

(Wheel spins.
 She goes to the wheel . . .)

You *know* how to do this!!!
Oh, a strong tide . . .

(With difficulty, she does . . .)

My lovely ship . . .
The wind, the tide and I will take you round this
 smelly island
And hide you for my friends!!!

(Wind quickens.
 Ship sails . . .)

EIGHT
I AM PIRATE

The goodies' camp . . .
 What looks like the sleeping (and in one case dead)
forms of Grey, Doctor, Captain, Silent Sue, Red Ruth.

Jim *(arrives triumphant)*
 Captain Hawkins here!
 Master Sailor!
 Through her *wide* knowledge of seafaring, her
  superhuman strength

And her *indomitable* courage . . .
Has anchored her *schooner* safe out of sight yonder!
I will wake my friends with this *wonderful* news . . .

(*It may be quite hard walking in wet trousers . . .
    Shoes squelch as . . . prodding, she thinks, Doctor.*)

Doctor Livesey?
Doctor . . . *wake up* . . . I have some good
Owwww!!!

(*Has the Doctor nipped her?
    She sees, hovering above the sleeping form . . .
    Two strange glowing lights.
    And she hears . . .*)

Flint

Who's this burnt-arsed whore?
Who's this burnt-arsed whore?
Who's this burnt-arsed whore????

(*A hand snakes out from the sleeping form, seizes her
ankle . . .*)

Silver

Oh Captain Flint, what *have* we here????
Torches, swabs!!!

(*And the sleeping forms transmogrify into a circle of
torch-carrying, grog-fuelled pirates . . .*)

So here's Jim Hawkins live as a basket of eels
Just in time to read for us.

Jim

You here????

Silver

And smart as paint!

Jim

This is *our* camp!!!
Where are *my friends*????

Silver
Your *friends* are not your friends no more

Jim
Liar!

Silver
Squire says 'That dog Jim has run off from us!'
The Doctor himself is dead set against you

Jim
No!

Silver
Oh dear me Yes!

Circle of Pirates
Oh dear me Yes!

Silver
'That Ungrateful Cowardly Scamp' he cries
'I can't think *why* I been so guarding of her
wretched little life. *She's* betrayed *us*
we might as well betray *her*
take our places gentlemen,
help yourselves to some tobacco

(*Circle of pirates lift their pipes.*)

Avail yourselves of some grog

(*Circle of pirates raise their grog.*)

Jim (*shouts*)
Squire!!!

(*Silence.*)

Doctor!!!

(*Silence.*)

Silver
See????
Skedaddled!
Doctor says
'You bested us and you are the better fellow so
   our brandy

(*Pirates lift their grog and drink.*)

our tobacco

(*Pirates smoke their pipes.*)

our vittles . . .

(*Pirates gnaw on barbecued chicken pieces . . .*)

our warm fire here.

(*Pirates each hold out a hand to the blaze . . .*)

is for *you*.'
And adds he
'Here is something just for *you*, Long John . . . '
And hands me *this*.

(*Silver dangles the map.*)

Jim
Our map!

Silver
My map.
Which you must read for us *Instanter* . . .

Jim
The doctor gave away our map????

Silver
Yes

Jim
To *you*????

Silver

Yes
He says
'Silver, you're the only swab among you as can *read*.
You are so quick of thought, Silver . . .
I'm for you!
'As for *that girl*' Doctor says . . .
Confound her!
Kill her drown her, Silver, I don't much care . . .
We're about *sick* of *her* . . .'
And so am I . . .
But *we're* not sick of you . . .
We need you to read our map

Jim

You read it!

Badger

Turns out he was *lying* about reading!

Silver

Exaggerating merely, George Badger!
Jim . . . we know you is smart as paint and can *read*

Jim

This world is more terrible than I could have imagined!
For my *friends* who I left *Grandma for* . . .
Have *deserted* me!!!
For *them*
I swam a *sea*!
I sailed *alone* a *ship*!
I fought a *man* while *they*
Give away the map I almost gave my *life* for!!!
I *hate* you, Squire!
I *double* hate *you*, Doctor!!!
I have nothing left to believe in but *treasure treasure
    treasure*
Give me the map.
I will be a pirate too!

Silver
　　Read the map, Pirate Girl.
　　Let's after treasure!

　　(*And all pirates gather admiringly about Jim.*)

Joan
　　I can do *reading* it's just *writing* don't never make
　　　　no *sense*!

Silver
　　Read!

Jim (*reads*)
　　'If I have *something*　　from my pile.
　　Lat E 62　*big bullet hole*　will find the isle . . .'
　　This *hole* someone shot through helps me not at all!

Badger
　　That was *you,* / Silver!

Silver
　　Coordinates coordinates to *here*! *We're here ain't*
　　　　we? Read round!

Jim　(*reads on*)
　　'The heart protected by the ribs
　　Who knows this will get his dibs
　　Upon it . . .'

Joan
　　That's *hard*.

Dick
　　We need to look for a skeleton . . .

Black Dog
　　Just like Flint to bury gold in a corpse . . .

　　(*He starts sniffing like a dog . . .*)

Silver
　　Good Dog, Find!

Dick
Search among and round of these . . .

(*They scour the bottom of the ribs . . .*)

Ribs ribs . . .

Jim
What do *these* put you in mind of . . .?

Joan
Ribs!
Smashed ribs dush dush and dush but ribs!!!

Lucky Micky
Where are we? . . .

Joan
Standing in the very ribs!

Lucky Micky
That's cos you're with Lucky Micky!!!!

Silver
Read *on* . . .

Jim
'If unfair of face
It's simple
Escalate the biggest pimple . . .'

Black Dog
Unfair of face?
We're all unfair of face!!

Dick
But who's *unfairest* of face . . .?

Joan
You!

Dick
No!!!
You!

Joan

Top o' my face is unfair but bottom of my face is
pretty!!

Jim

This landscape . . . looked from on high . . .
It would look . . .

Silver

Like a great round face . . .
Covered in . . .

Jim

Stubble and . . .

Silver

Spots!!!

(*And they find . . .*)

Jim

Biggest pimple!

Silver

Escalate it!!!

(*They all escalate it . . .*)

Jim

'Upon that spot I suggest you linger . . .'

Dick

Quickly . . . sun's going down . . .
Shadows is stretching . . .

(*They stand . . . It is crowded . . .*)

Jim

'Until you see a pointing finger . . .'

Silver

Nothing!

Badger
> Linger!
> It said we have to *linger*!!!

> (*They all linger . . .*)

Joan
> Lingering drives me . . . dushdushdush dush . . .

> (*And linger omnes, until . . . in the beautiful and quick
> tropical sunset . . .*
> *Gleaming through a hole in a rib . . . a ray of dying
> sun picks out . . .*
> *A shadow from one of the ribs lengthen like a finger,
> pointing to . . . a glowing circle!*)

Silver
> *Look!!!!*

Jim
> That looks like . . . a cross . . .

Mutineers
> X marks the spot X spots the spot it's the treasure!!!!!

> (*They dig but find only . . .*)

Dick
> Piece o' whalebone! Words scrimshawed on it!!

Joan
> Not more *reading*!!!!

Silver
> I can almost *smell* treasure. Read On!!!

Jim
> 'Stand thereupon
> Chose moon or sun
> The cove as knows to turn his face
> Has wit and luck to find the place,
> By my hand. Edward Flint.'

(*All, rooted, turn their faces this way and that, very alert, like meerkats . . . as if some treasure might trundle out and fall at their feet.*
   They are all looking left, right, down . . .)

Badger
   More lingering . . .
   It's really not fair . . .

(*No one is looking up, as stars appear.*)

Jim
   'By my hand, Edward Flint.'

(*And she looks up at the stars . . .*
   Sees something . . . right above where we want it . . .)

   Look . . .

Black Dog
   Nothing! Very *Nothing*.

Joan
   Just *darkness*.
   Dush!!!!

Jim
   Up there
   Those stars . . .
   What shape is that . . .????

Joan
   A *fist*!

Black Dog
   FLINT'S FIST!!!!!

Badger
   His very finger pointing . . .

Silver
   Flint's PILE!!!!

(And they all rush with spades and picks. They dig furiously . . .
    Until . . . a clang . . .)

Badger
    Something *hard* here!

(They sink their hands elbow deep in the pustule.
    Bring out . . .
    Something wrapped in a HUGE hat.)

Dick
    That's Grimes' *Hat!*

Joan
    Tied with something long and yellow . . .

Dick
    Allardyce's lovely hair!

Badger
    I don't like this!

Silver
    Cut it!!!

(They cut it . . . reveal . . . a music box.)

Black Dog
    O'Doherty's music box!!!!

Silver
    Open it!!!

Lucky Micky *(whispers)*
    Fingers crossed!!!

(They open it . . .
    It plays a tinkly 'Fifteen men on a dead man's chest' refrain . . .
    Walrus crew extremely spooked . . .)

Badger
I don't like this at all!

Silver
What's *that*??????

Joan
Little boy sailor there . . . twirling . . .

(*All intake breath.*)

Black Dog
It's the very spit o' that chimney sweep cabin boy as
was such a pet of yours, Barbecue . . .

Several
Ben Gunn!!!!

Joan
One o' they six as this island *disappeared* . . .

(*Oooh scary* . . .)

Dick
Suppose he's turned *ghost*?????
Oooh, very scary . . .

Jim (*looks closely at it, it's a bit familiar*)
It's holding a piece of parchment . . .

Silver
I seen dead men I never seen a dead *boy*
Read it!

Jim
'For those who've felt both wounds and hurts . . .'

Badger
That's *us!*

Blackdog
That's very *us!*

Jim

'You now enjoy your just deserts.'

Silver

Our treasure!!!

Jim

'You've found the box, you've followed the map
You need now to ope your trap!' . . .
I am growing weary of reading this terrible verse . . .

Silver

Read on!

Jim

'To stuff those groats
Into your coats
Right up to their gunnels
Try and find a maze of tunnels.'

Silver

Trap!

(Pirates scrabble testing for traps.
  Tapping is sharp until . . .)

Joan

Shush!

(They all shush . . .
  She tries . . .)

Dush . . .

(The 'Dush' echoes and reverberates, like it is above.
Finds . . .)

Trap!

(Opens it . . .)

Maze of tunnels.
  And they descend into . . .

I AM NOT PIRATE

A maze of underground tunnels . . .
Pirates go all gold-fever-frenzied digging . . .
They lay down their weapons above ground . . .
scrabble and search . . .
Running hither and thither, disappearing and
reappearing from the tunnels . . .

Black Dog
I'll take this tunnel!

Dick
I this

Joan
I this!

Lucky Micky
This one looks lucky!

Badger
It's not fair . . . I haven't got my own tunnel!

(*The Parrot Flint settles somewhere and watches with*
interest . . .)

Silver
Yes!
Search, swabs!
If only I could be up those nooks and crannies along
of you all
But a one-legged man is no help in *holes*!
(*Whispers.*) Jim, come closer . . .
Can I trust you?

Jim
As much as *I* can trust *you*, Long John.

Silver
Stay up here by the trap, Girl . . . here.

(*Silver hands Jim a pistol . . .*
   Jim looks at the pistol, looks at Silver . . .)

Didn't think I'd play ill by my Cabin Girl did you?
See how I *trust* you . . .?
With my *life*
We let these worms wriggle and burrow . . .
As soon as we see 'em start up the ladder with the loot
You and Me . . . we puts a pistol ball in every one o'
   their brains!
Me . . . Black Dog then . . . the Goat . . .
You . . . Badger . . . Dick . . . the Girl . . .
Not so Lucky this time Micky . . .
Then . . . treasure's *ours,* Darling.
Two shares.
Bigger than seven shares.
Adds up, doesn't it?
Pure Mathematics, isn't it!

(*Offers pistol again.*)

Take it.

(*Jim takes it.*)

Clever girl!
You stand here . . .
I'll stand there . . .

(*And moves to prime position . . .*)

Very soon
Subtraction for *them*
Multiplication for *us*!
Such riches as will be ours!

(*Silver takes up a position, concealed pistol ready . . .*)

The things you can buy for Grandma!
Hens Numerous!
Chairs Comfortable!
Cottages, one for *Her* but a *Castle* for you!

Jim (*looks at the pistol*)

> *Grandma* . . . wouldn't take a penny that wasn't hers!
> Even when she was *starving* even when *I* was
>   starving!!!
> 'My dues and not a farthing more!'
> Oh Jim, you *fool*, Grandma would HATE you if you
>   were a pirate!
> *You're Jim Hawkins,*
> *Granddaughter to Grandma Hawkins!!!!!*
> An *honest* girl from Black Cove , England
> Noo *pirate*!!!!!!!!!!!!!!!!

> (*Delightful thought . . .*)

> But someone who has
> A *Pistol* from a Lying Pirate!!!
> *Which is delicious!!!*

> (*All pirates emerge from the tunnels and holes they*
> *have been searching.*)

Black Dog
> Nothing here!

Dick
> Or here

Joan
> Or here

Badger
> No rainbow's end no crock of gold . . .

Lucky Micky
> I've found another piece of parchment!!!

Silver
> More clues!!!

Lucky Micky
> No clues . . .
> Just . . . this . . .

(*Shows the BLACK SPOT.*
   Terrible silence.)

Badger

There's no treasure here.
Just the Black Spot.

(*It is very very scary . . .*)

Where our fine 'leader' led us.
Our 'Captain Silver'.
This is a poor pass you brought us to here, Silver
A very poor pass . . .

Silver

Swabs!
Villains!
We followed Flint's map, didn't we?
Treasure's down here . . .
You Lags and Lollards is too lazy to explore every
   maze end!!

(*He puts his gun down.*)

A poor one-legged man leads you right to the treasure
Now a poor one-legged man has to jump down into
   a pit
And do the uncovering hisself!!

(*And slides into the cave.*)

Hand me a marlinspike!!!

Badger

I *tell* you . . . there's *nothing* not a *groat* not a *sou*.

Silver

And I tell *you* keep looking!

Black Dog

And I tell *you look* and *spike* and *pick* and command
   all you like
There is no treasure here!!!

163

(*And they crowd Silver as . . .*)

Jim (*points her pistol*)
And *I* tell *you*
Drop your spades and picks
I am arresting you in the name of . . . justice and . . .
Not *lying*
Surrender yourselves to me now
And I will take you back to England for fair trial!

Silver
Well . . .
You has *bested* us.
We need a fine fierce captain like *Captain Flint*
To get us out of this new hole!
Bird

Flint (*lands on Jim*)
Oh you knackleass
Oh you fartleberry
Oh you madge!!!

(*And knocks Jim's pistol into Silver's hand . . .
Silver Points it at Jim.*)

Silver
Oh you foolish misguided girl!

(*Cocks it.*)

Wrong side of the equation again!!!

TEN
A REAL GHOST!

A sound of bones.
A rush of wind.
A terrible, frightening voice . . .

Voice
    Pay heed to the Black Spot!
    I send you the Black Spot
    And you *Proceed?????*
    Who steals *my treasure?*

    (*It stops everyone dead.*)

    Who steals my treasure?

Dick
    Oh dear God, what's that????

Joan
    It's *the Island* speaking!!!

Voice
    Edward Flint asks
    Who steals my treasure????

All
    It's Flint!!!!

Voice
    Who steals my treasure???

Silver
    I do, Captain!

Voice
    Call you me *Captain,*
    After you put your arm round my shoulder like *a
        friend* . . .
    Then plunged your dagger one two three times
    Into my back you murderer??!!!

Dick
    Oh dear Lord . . . it's *Flint*!!!

Silver
    Then, Captain, you're dead . . .
    I placed the pennies on your vacant staring *deadlights*!

Voice

Yet here I am, floating in the dark very near you . . .

Silver

Aaaaghnodon'tcomenearmedon'tcomenearme!!!

Voice

At the very corner of you . . .

Silver

Not again!

Voice

Long John Silver so you see me *not* each and every
night in the dark by your bunk . . .
You must do my bidding must you not!

Silver (*terrified*)

Yes, Captain Ghost!

Voice

Black Dog . . .

(*Black Dog goes rigid with terror.*)

Black Dog

Yes Captain!!!!

Voice

George Badger

(*Ditto George Badger. Incapable of speech, he multi-
nods.*)

Dick the Dandy

(*Ditto Dick the Dandy.*)

Dick

Even in death *he sees us*!

Voice

Joan the Goat

166

Joan

Even in death he knows our very names!

Voice

Even in *Death* I am your *Captain* you are still my
   crew and I *command* you!!!

All

Yes Captain Flint????

Voice

This island killed *not* your friends Allardyce, McGraw,
O'Doherty,
Thimble Grimes the giant and the chimley sweep cabin
   boy . . .
The villain *Silver* killed them
Seize the villain Silver!!!
You too NotNowSoLucky Micky!!!

All

Aye aye Captain Flint!

(*They all grab on to Silver.*)

Various

We got him, Captain! Aye aye! He's seized! Aye aye!!!
The villain Silver is seized, Captain!
What do you want us to do with the villain Captain???

Voice

Clap him in irons!

All

Aye aye Captain!!!

Silver

Just a moment!

(*All stop.*)

Lucky Micky was never crew member to *you* . . .
   Captain . . .

Voice

Not in *life* perhaps . . . Do not *quibble* with a ghost, Sir!!!

Silver

Did you say *chimley* boy . . . Ghost?

Voice

Chimney I said *chimney* boy, Mortal . . . *Blaggard!!!*

Silver

Well   *Ghost* . . .
After these swabs has clapped *me* in irons . . .
What then?

(*Silence.*)

Captain Flint . . . ?

(*Silence.*

Silver waits, smiling nicely . . .
Jim looks around . . .
From all directions along the tunnels . . . he sees
Doctor, Grey, Silent Sue and Ben Gunn climbing
towards them, pistols in one hand, burning torches in
the other . . .
Doctor puts one finger to lips . . . with the other
points to where, concealed, crouches the Squire with
a large conch . . .)

Silver

What then . . .
After the swabs has clapped *me* in irons
O *dread* and *dead* Captain Flint . . .????

Voice (*losing it*)

Then they will clap themselves in irons and I will
   march every villain among you back to England to
   stand fair trial for the cold-blooded murder of my
   ploughwoman!! Then hang by your extraordinarily
   filthy throats until You Are Dead!!!

(*Silence.*)

Silver
Anything else . . . *Squire Stupid?*???

Ben Gunn
BenGunn*said*hewouldn'tstayincharacterdidn'tyou
    BenGunnyesIdid!

Doctor
He *swore* he was *good* at *Theatricals!!!*
Charge!!!!

Silver
Kill!

ELEVEN
A REAL FIGHT

Squire
Capture every last rascal!!!

(*All baddies disappear into the three holes . . .
    Followed by all goodies but Doctor and Jim . . .*)

Doctor
Stand by a hole, Jim.
We may *thwack* them as they emerge . . .

Jim
You gave Silver the map!

Doctor
Because Ben Gunn came and told us where he'd
    hidden the treasure!

Jim
But there's no treasure

Squire
Oh but there is!!!

(*Ben Gunn emerges from a hole. They almost thwack him as . . .*)

Ben Gunn

Ben Gunn moved the treasure!!!BenGunnthinksI'll moveandhidethat treasuremakeitmineallminejust likefalseSilverwouldalso

I'vespentthreeyearswithnocheeseandnothingtodoIthought whydon'tjusttputthetreasuresomewhereelse!!!

(*Black Dog emerges from some hole.*)

(*Doctor thwacks him.*)

Doctor

Sack Ben Gunn!

Ben Gunn

SackfunnyDoctorPerson!

Doctor

And *chimney,* not *chimley*!!!

(*Puts sack over Black Dog.
Meanwhile . . .
Lucky Micky emerges.*)

Lucky Micky

Oh *no* weapon!
Look on the floor!

(*Nothing!*)

Pockets!

(*Nothing!*)

Luck's run out!

(*A pit-prop or something falls right into his arms.*)

Still Lucky Micky!!!

(*But he is felled by a cosh from behind.
Falls to reveal . . .*)

Grey

I might *finally* have found a career that suits my
personality . . .
Grey the *Grey Pursuer!!!*

(*He runs into a tunnel for another baddie . . .
Dick emerges from tunnel . . . sees Ben Gunn.*)

Dick

You're f*amiliar, ill-dressed* villain! Agh!!!
You're our *cabin boy* villain!!!

Ben Gunn

NotnomoreI'mnot!!!!
I'm Chimley Man!!!

(*And disappears!
Doctor bops Dick.*)

Doctor

And you're Captured, Dandy!
Sack, Jim!

Jim

Sack, Doctor.

(*They both place sack over Dick and sit him next to
Black Dog as . . .*)

Doctor

Did you like my ditty, Jim?

Jim

What ditty?

Doctor

In the music box!

(*Ben Gunn emerges from a tunnel, chased by Joan . . .*)

Ben Gunn

Ben Gunn's idea!
ScareLongJohnSilverforallthetimeshescaredme!!!

Doctor

Boy's self-educated . . . says 'chimley' doesn't
understand *scansion*. Too many syllables but clever
rhymes . . .

(*Doctor tries to whack Joan on the head. Clang!
Sprains wrist.*)

Ow!

Ben Gunn

Muther!!!!

(*Joan, unhurt, chases Ben Gunn down another tunnel.
Silver, pursued by Squire emerges from a different
tunnel.
Doctor whacks him.*)

Squire

At last your Just Deserts, Former Friend!!!

(*Silver goes down.*)

Silver

How I do hate *Good* People and *Poetic Justice*!!!!!

(*Jim, Doctor and Squire bag him, put him with others.
As . . .*)

Squire

We have their leader subdued and secured!!!!
The fight will soon go out of his cohorts!!!

(*Joan and Silent Sue fall out of a tunnel, belying this
opinion . . .
Doctor, Squire and Jim try to cosh right head . . .
but one is a goody head, the other covered in a
stewpot lid . . .
Following two speeches intermingled . . .*)

Joan

Ahyerscreamingbleedingdamnationdevilwoman
whirlingdervishblitheringbanshee!!!

Silent Sue
Ayyyeeeeeeeyaghhhhhwargghhhhhfarghhhgarfffffff!!!

(*As Squire, Doctor and Jim have succeeded in getting Joan the Goat by at least three of her limbs . . .*)

Squire
We've got her . . .

(*They sort of haven't . . .*)

Joan
Awyerswinesyervillainsyerbrigandsyerbeesyerweevils yer worms!!!

(*Sue gets the fourth errant limb . . . They pin her down and bag her.
   Badger emerges backwards from a tunnel . . .
   Shouting down the hole . . .*)

Badger
Escaped yer, didn't I?
I've found a safe cave here!

(*He turns round, sees he hasn't . . .*)

It's not fair!

(*Doctor coshes him. He's bagged as . . .*)

Doctor
That's all of the blackhearted rascals.

Squire
Then, Hear Me!
I am a *magistrate*, Sirs
You are, every man jack of you, under my arrest!
You are all in my power
Including *you*, Long John Silver . . .

(*Takes sack off him.
   It is Grey.*)

Who the *devil* are you?

Grey
> Grey Sir, GREYGREYGREY!!!
> Call yourselves shipmates!!!
> Not *one* of you noticed Silver turn to Grey, not one
> of you!!!!

Doctor
> Where the *hell* is Silver?

Silver (*appears from a tunnel*)
> After his Treasure still!
> Mine!
> Where / Damme *where*?????

Ben Gunn
> Don't bang! don't wallop Island doesn't like banging
> and walloping!!!

> (*Island groans . . . wobbles . . .*)

> It starts shifting and complaining!!!

> (*It mutters and complains . . .*)

> I put it where it it works like Flint's chest The treasure
> isn't in the bottom
> The treasure's in the . . .

Silver
> Treasure . . . *Come to me!!!*

Ben Gunn
> In *the chimley* . . .

> (*The ceiling collapses.*
> *Treasure buries and engulfs Silver.*)

Jim
> No!!!!!!

> (*Jim tries frantically to dig him out . . .*)

> Long John!
> Silver!

(*But finds only his lifeless hand, clutching one of two coins of low denomination . . .*
   The Parrot flutters down, lands on Silver's hand for a moment.)

Flint (*laughs cruelly, aping Silver's laugh*)
   Pieces of eight!
   Pieces of eight!
   Hehehehehe!

   (*Disappears.*)

Doctor (*a bit Greta Garbo in 'Queen Christina'*)
   What blood and sorrow
   What good ships scuttled in the deep
   What brave men walking the plank blindfold

Ben Gunn
   Yes . . .

Doctor
   Shot of cannon
   Flash of cutlass
   Thrust of dagger
   Shame and lies and cruelty . . .

Ben Gunn
   Yes

Doctor
   For what?
   For gold. Hard, shiny, cold dead gold

Ben Gunn
   Seethisisthetruecharacteroftreasurecoldhearted
      dangerousandnotusefulordeliciouslikeachimley
      systemoreatablelikecheese . . .

Squire
   Friends
   We are stranded on this terrible island

(*Silent Sue sobs loudly . . .*)

But we are alive
Silent Sue . . . we are *alive*

Doctor

Silent Sue . . . *shhhhhh!*

Squire

We must learn to live together somehow . . .
I will be in charge . . .
The island's *Squire* if you will

Jim

Squire . . .

Squire

We will learn to *plough* and *plant* and grow our food
in this wretched landscape . . .

Jim

Squire –

Squire

We will be happy here

Jim

Squire, I have the ship secure and moored beyond
that headland . . .

Squire

Oh thank heaven for that, collect up all that lovely
sparkling gold and
Board Ship!
To England!!!

(*And the terrible island disappears as . . .*)

TWELVE
I NEVER WILL BE A WILD ROVER NO MORE

Song: Homeward Bound (Shanty Man and company)

It's time to go now,
Haul away the anchor
Haul away the anchor
'Tis our sailing time
'Tis our sailing time

Get some sail upon her
Haul away the halyard
Haul away the halyard
'Tis our sailing time
'Tis our sailing time

When my body's grounded
Haul away to Heaven
Haul away to Heaven
God be by my side
On the evening tide
'Tis our sailing time

THIRTEEN
A CHAIR BY A FIRESIDE

And the Admiral Benbow Inn appears . . .
Grandma serving a solitary Mrs Crossley.

Grandma
My H-A-R-T aches
A-K-E-S
My granddaughter
My Jimima!!!
Named by *me*
J-I-M-I-M-A
My J-I-M!!!!
Another Ladies' Delight, Mrs Crossley?

Mrs Crossley

Just a tiny one, Mrs Hawkins . . .

Grandma

Small water for your laying hen also . . .?

Mrs Crossley

Just a tiny one . . .

(*Grandma exits for drinks . . .*
Jim walks in with shell-encrusted chair . . .
Also Squire and Ben Gunn and Doctor . . .
Jim and Doctor Livesey are both in very fine
dresses . . . in which they have some difficulty in
walking . . .)

Jim

Grandma?! Grandma!

I'm back and we're *rich* and we're going to rescue
chimney sweeps –

(*Clearly the voyage home has been rich with debate . . .*)

– and open schools for them and use wealth for good
not greed and . . .

Gone!!!!!

Not dead??!! Oh, I should never have left her!!!

(*Grandma walks in with a glass of brandy . . .*)

Grandma

Jim?

Jim in a lovely *dress*!

Jim!!!!

(*Tearful reunion.*
Grandma sees Doctor.)

Someone *else* in a lovely dress . . .????

Doctor Livesey?????

Doctor *Livesey* in a lovely dress??????

Doctor
These things are hopeless for *work*

Jim
These things are hopeless for adventures

Jim / Doctor
Hopeless!!!

Doctor
Tonight . . .
Finery   Fun   Fol de rol
First thing tomorrow . . .

Both
Back in the breeches
To do good works with all our gold!!!

(*Grandma sees Ben Gunn.*)

Grandma
What in the devil's hell *is that*?

Ben Gunn
I'mBenGunnIamareyou (*Nips.*) A RealGrandma???

Doctor
No nipping no / nipping!!!

Grandma
I need a brandy I do
From the *special* barrel . . .

Ben Gunn
With some nice cheese?

Squire
We will drink to pernicious Pirates justly Punished
And a long and happy life . . .
turning Bad to Better . . .
and *Gold* to *Good*
and, modest drinks of choice all round . . .

Jim

I was *home.*
H O A M, Grandma!
With *cheese*!
Which we can *eat*
With *gold* which we *cannot*!
My tale is told.
My ship returned.
Oxen and wain ropes would not bring me back to
That *accursed* island.
Now . . .
The worst nightmares that ever I have
Are when I hear the surf booming about its coasts
Or start upright in bed
Hearing

Flint

Pieces of eight
Pieces of eight
Pieces of eight
You burned-arsed madge!

(*They all look round, terrified . . .*)

Curtain.